A MANUAL:
CREATING AN AUTISM
INTERVENTION PROGRAM

Tameika N. Meadows, M.Ed., BCBA

DEDICATION

This book is dedicated to the parents I have worked side by side, and shoulder to shoulder with over the years who have taught me about the difficulties, sadness, fears, joys, and celebrations of raising a child with Autism. **You are rock stars!** The success stories you share, the tears you shed, the frustrations that you vent, and the questions you ask, encourage me to do my job better and better each day.

"At the end of knowledge, wisdom begins, and at the end of wisdom, there is not grief...but hope".

Lloyd Alexander

Introduction

"*A Manual: Creating an Autism Intervention Program*" is intended to be an introductory instructional guide and resource for people in underserved areas lacking qualified support, specialized training, and knowledge. I would love it if every Autism program or intervention center had access to qualified and experienced staff, but unfortunately that is not always the case.

Think of this manual as a How To guide, complete with strategies, tips, and plenty of sample resources (if you want to start printing off resources now, flip straight to the **Appendix** section in the back of the book!). This manual is best used for setting up and operating a day program or center based facility for children with Autism or related Developmental Disorders, based in Applied Behavior Analysis (ABA) methodology. A "day program" is my general term for any type of center, organization, residential facility, private school, charter school, Pre-K program, or social skills group that seeks to teach skills and improve the lives of individuals with Autism.

My career began by working with severely underserved families without access to local professionals or local expertise. Bringing in experts can be difficult, expensive, and time consuming. You may live in an area with no or a minimal amount of ABA professionals or maybe you cannot afford the individualized services of an ABA professional.

This manual is intended to serve as a facilitator for individuals in need of quality services, and to provide a basic foundation of knowledge that can be modified to fit your particular needs. **This manual is by no means intended to be a substitute for the professional help of a qualified Board Certified Behavior Analyst or a Board Certified Assistant Behavior Analyst.** Rather, this manual is a stepping stone for individuals and communities with children in need of specialized instruction and behavioral management, who have dire needs that are not currently being met in your local community.

The information and recommendations in this manual are not narrow or restrictive. Feel free to adapt the information to fit the needs of your agency, program, or school. The recommendations in this manual are derived from my years of experience teaching children with Autism, my specialized ABA training, and also direct work experience in successful Autism centers or day programs. Think of this manual as a template, and then take that template and make it applicable to your program or facility.

The enclosed information can also be helpful for school systems, in-home programs, or ABA Consultants who work with clients in isolated areas such as small rural communities or international locations. This information is suitable for use with multiple disabilities, and can be placed in the hands of anyone responsible for setting up or running an Autism program. That could include a School Director, Center Program Manager, BCBA, BCaBA, Lead ABA Therapist, Lead Teacher, Group Home Leader, Principal, Social Group Coordinator, ABA therapist, or a parent.

My personal motto when it applies to teaching and training is to be *Simple, Relatable, & Practical,* and I hope you will agree that this manual embodies all 3 of these traits.

It is my sincere hope that with the consistent use of this manual, individuals and communities will be motivated into action to begin providing quality ABA services to children in need, and to delve further into an understanding of the science of ABA. ABA can bring about amazing changes and success in the lives of individuals with Developmental Disabilities, and I have seen it happen many, many times.

Good Luck!

TABLE OF CONTENTS

CLIENT POPULATION

First things first: *who are the consumers that the day program will help?*

ABA therapy is mostly known as a behavioral intervention for children with Autism that typically occurs inside of homes. However ABA is much bigger than Autism. Individuals with learning needs, traumatic brain injury, severe behavioral challenges, developmental deficits, mental retardation, or issues with attending, daily functioning, or generalizing skills, can all potentially benefit from ABA services. Even typically developing children exhibiting behavioral issues who aren't fitting in well to general education classrooms could potentially benefit from a day program or clinic based intervention, although they likely wouldn't need to attend as long as a child with a disability.

Although most ABA professionals travel to clients homes to provide therapy services, more and more clinic based facilities are opening up and appearing in communities. So which treatment method is best? Well, current research indicates that both clinic based ABA treatment and home based ABA treatment can bring about significant and lasting improvements in the lives of individuals with Autism (Eikeseth, 2009).

Clinic based treatment has multiple advantages over home based services, such as peers are readily available for social interaction goals, instructional control can be easier to achieve, and the environment can be better modified and adapted to suit the needs of the children (needs that often change and shift over time). A big advantage of a clinic based treatment modality for staff and professionals is being able to brainstorm, generate ideas and creativity, and connect with other professionals *in the moment*, as this isn't possible in a home based modality. I have personally found this advantage to be very helpful in day programs, when I can just walk across the hall to pick the brain of another ABA professional.

Day programs often appeal to families who do not have access to specialized toys, materials, or equipment in their home, or who want their child to receive 1:1 therapy in a setting that resembles school (to make the transition into school much easier later on).

So the first step when creating a day program or ABA intervention center is to decide how narrow of a focus the day program should have. There are many factors to consider including:

-<u>Funding sources</u>: How will the day program be funded? By the state? By the government? Through grants? Through scholarships? Will the day program accept private insurance? Often the funding source will dictate who can receive treatment, and it is common that if insurance is involved then the children will need an actual diagnosis, and the diagnosis may have to be an Autistic Spectrum Disorder (ASD). On the other hand, if the funding source is the government or the state then they may want the day program to serve a wide range of diverse clients. If the funding source is private pay (parents pay out of pocket) then individuals without an actual diagnosis can easily receive treatment, which would be helpful for parents who may not have access to diagnosticians. While opening up the day program to a wider clientele will be a great help to the community and to families that also means that a more diversified and experienced staff will be necessary. Not all professionals have experience with a wide array of disorders or disabilities, so it will be important to provide high quality and ongoing staff training.

-<u>Community need</u>: This would require gathering information about the needs of the children living in the community. Is there a large Autism population? Is there a large ADHD population? Does the community lack centers with a behavioral approach to treatment? The present need will help determine what populations to serve. In underserved rural or international areas it can be very difficult to locate a professional qualified to diagnose developmental disabilities. For this reason, requiring children accepted into the day program to have a specific diagnosis could unintentionally make the day program inaccessible to the families who need the most help. It's important to try and help as many children as possible, while still maintaining quality. If the day program does not have the space or resources to accommodate a specific disability or need (such as an entrance ramp for children in wheelchairs), it is better to decline those clients or refer them to other programs than to lower the quality of services.

-<u>Staff available</u>: What background and experience does the available staff possess? Is it possible to bring in qualified staff from other states or countries? If the day program offers services to adolescents and adults, is the staff trained in physical management and safety? If the day program offers services to toddlers, is the staff trained in early intervention and the socio-emotional development of young children? Is the staff to child ratio high enough to accept different age groups into the day program? Children with large gaps in age should not be lumped together (such as a 3 year old taught with an 8 year old). If the day program will accept a wide range of ages, then there needs to be enough staff available to ensure safety and quality of instruction. A lack of quality, experienced staff may limit the amount of children who can be served and the **severity** of children that can be served. For example, if the day program does not have access to a competent BCBA, then it's highly discouraged that the day program accepts highly aggressive children who exhibit high rates of harmful behaviors towards others or themselves. For this reason, some day programs choose to set policies about behavioral and functioning level requirements for a child to participate in the program. For example, some centers may state that children must have a certain IQ or higher and be verbal in order to enroll.

After considering the above factors, a decision needs to be made about what populations of clients can best be served at the day program. Regardless of disability or diagnosis, if a child can be helped by the services provided at the day program then they should be allowed to participate, even if only on a part time basis.

It is recommended that staff to child ratios be kept very low, with 1:1 being preferred. The ability to provide 1:1 intensive instruction that is modified to the learner is a part of providing quality ABA instruction. Often children with Autism may get overwhelmed or overly distracted when even 1-2 peers are added to the environment, or if group attending is required. Another advantage of 1:1 instruction is the child and the teacher will grow to have a close and paired relationship, where the teacher becomes adept at recognizing the child's strengths and weaknesses and can anticipate when to modify the curriculum, when to increase difficulty of tasks, etc.

Beyond just having ABA experience, it is recommended that staff have experience working with a wide range of disabilities and challenges, such as Autism, Downs Syndrome, feeding difficulties, or Attention Deficit Disorder. This will allow the day program to have individuals of varying competencies and expertise all joining together to come up with teaching strategies, motivation techniques, and organizational ideas. You don't want to be one of those ABA professionals who "doesn't play well with others".

I have worked in many types of settings over the years, and the work settings I enjoyed the most were diverse and collaborative, with people of varying experience and training brainstorming on the best way to teach an individual child. Working side by side with professionals who come from early interventionist backgrounds, or medical backgrounds, or counseling backgrounds, allows for open collaboration and sharing of different worldviews.

POLICIES & PROCEDURES

"P&P" should be the next major business decisions made after determining what population the day program will serve. The development of P&P will determine the rules, boundaries, guidelines, and responsibilities of the day center and sharing this information with families during the intake process, as well as with all employees, can help to reduce potential conflict or miscommunications further down the road. It's always a good idea to start a relationship with any new client by defining the limits of the therapeutic relationship; this is true whether you see your client in a home, classroom, or day program.

The P&P of the day program should be aimed at answering "What If?" questions.

What If...

- **A child is brought to the day center who is clearly ill?**
- **A parent is 2 hours late picking up a child?**
- **An employee is emotionally abusive towards a child?**
- **One employee is sexually harassing another employee?**
- **A child wanders outside of the building and gets hurt?**
- **An employee is badly bitten by a child?**
- **A person arrives at the center to pick up a child, but the parents have not signed consent for that person?**
- **An employee discovers bad bruises on the back of a child?**
- **An employee regularly sends and receives text messages throughout the work day?**
- **An employee posts photos of a client on their personal blog or website?**
- **A parent tries to "steal away" an employee to work for them privately?**

If you have spent the time preparing these policies in advance then if issues such as these arise, everyone should have a procedure to follow. The moment <u>after</u> a situation or emergency happens is not the time to create a policy on how to handle it. Without having P&P in place, employees may mishandle critical situations, or the day program could face liability. Having clear policies in place also protects all persons involved (staff and clients) from unfair or preferential treatment. The rules and guidelines should be clear and firm, even though management retains the right to modify P&P if necessary.

When working for companies who fail to adequately create P&P, I have often observed that staff satisfaction tends to be low. This is because when problems and conflicts occur, staff turns to management expecting a resolution. Without proper P&P in place, the management then wastes hours, days, or even weeks, discussing and coming up with how to handle situations while the staff must continue seeing the client and being in that awkward situation. Or, the management gives no answers or assistance to staff, and individual employees are left to determine how best to wade through awkward or ethically murky situations. Unhappy staff with low job satisfaction will lead to high staff turnover, and ultimately it is the children who suffer when staff habitually quit.

P&P will always be determined by the needs and culture of the specific work setting. I have worked for some centers with just a few rules, and other centers with a 50 page employee manual. Typically, you want the P&P to be a fluid process that is open to changes and modifications as issues arise. It isn't possible to think of every staff/employer, staff/staff, client/staff, client/employer conflict that could occur, so it is best to start with a brief template and then modify it over the years as needed. To provide a starting point, here is a sample list of important situations or events to address in the P&P of any day program or ABA clinic.

Sample Policies & Procedures List:

- Mission Statement & Company Vision
- Chain of Command (include contact information)
- Staff Job Descriptions
- Staff Rules of Conduct
- Staff Performance Evaluations

- Orientation/Training procedures
- Staff & Client Sick Policy
- Client Informed Consent
- Client Release of Information
- Requesting Days Off
- Anti-Discrimination Policy
- Vacation Pay/Overtime Policy
- Raise/Promotion Policy
- Benefits
- Transporting Clients Liability form
- No Compete/Non-Disclosure form
- Holidays/Center Closings
- Staff & Client Late Policy
- Dress Code
- Disciplinary Policies for insubordination, failure to report to work, etc.
- Staff & Client Accident & Injury forms
- Staff & Client Emergency Contact form
- Cell Phone Use
- Ethical Considerations/Confidentiality/HIPAA compliance
- Smoking/Drug Use/Alcohol Use policy
- Visitors Policy
- Mandatory Reporting Procedures (child abuse or child neglect)

METHODOLOGY/FOUNDATION

What does it mean to have Applied Behavior Analysis as the foundation and methodological basis for the day program?

It means that the day program has made a commitment to utilizing empirically sound methods and strategies to teach children, the fundamental principles of ABA will guide programming and instruction, and staff will pursue excellence by staying abreast of changes and advances to the field of ABA, in order to be most effective at their jobs.

In a more practical sense, having an ABA foundation will affect the way the day program teaches, monitors progress, handles challenging behaviors, and modifies instruction to suit the individual child.

A day program that is founded on ABA principles must incorporate the **Seven Dimensions of ABA.** The Seven Dimensions, created by Baer, Wolf, & Risley (1968), can help to determine if a program or intervention is sound and rooted in ABA methodology. If your day program is not encompassing the Seven Dimensions, then it cannot truly be called an ABA program.

1. Applied- The work conducted must have social significance.
2. Behavioral-Precise and reliable measurement of behavior should be attainable.
3. Analytic-It must be shown that the treatment led to behavior change, and not something else, such as chance.
4. Technological-Procedures should improve be clearly described and identified.
5. Conceptually Systematic-Procedures should be described in terms of their principles.
6. Effective-Procedures should improve the behaviors being addressed to a practical degree.
7. Generalized-Positive changes should extend over time, environments, and behaviors.

Below are several ABA teaching principles that would help any day program stand apart as a leader of excellence, in providing instruction to children with Autism. Incorporating these strategies into your day program is highly recommended:

ABA Principle: Reinforcement - All children should be motivated to learn based on the specific interests of that child. Internal as well as external rewards would be used so that children would have fun learning and enjoy school. Any time a child displayed learning difficulties or showed disinterest in learning, their reinforcement package should be re-evaluated for effectiveness and potency.

ABA Principle: Differentiated Instruction- Children should have a modified curriculum based on how they learn best. Some children may write vocabulary words on the chalkboard, while other children might type their vocabulary words on the classroom computer. It would depend on the way each individual child learns. Children should not be required to adapt to the curriculum; the curriculum should be modified to fit the child.

ABA Principle: Environment is Key to Understanding Behavior- Children displaying behavioral issues are not be viewed as "bad", or stubborn. The environment, such as teaching style, reinforcement, or an over-stimulating classroom, should be closely examined to look for factors maintaining poor behaviors. Problem behaviors should be analyzed using a Functional Behavior Assessment or Functional Analysis, and a qualified professional (a BCBA is recommended) must oversee all behavioral interventions. When dealing with a child who isn't making progress, the *ICEL Method* should be used to determine the problem. ICEL stands for "Instructor, Curriculum, Environment, Learner". The child is the last option to consider when learning problems happen.

ABA Principle: Analysis of Data- Ongoing data analysis should be part of all curriculum so staff will know when a student needs new challenges or might need simpler tasks. Children should be placed in specific learning tracks or grouped with other learners based on performance data and individual need, and not based on administration preferences, or teacher opinion. This focus on not just collecting, but actually analyzing data would lead to higher accountability for staff and administration, and better ease of reporting specific progress to families.

<u>ABA Principle: Prompting & Fading</u>- Prompting should be used to move a child from not knowing a skill, to knowing a skill. Prompt levels would vary depending on how much help the child needs, and reinforcement would increase as prompts decreased to encourage the child to desire to complete the task independently. All staff should be trained in using various prompting tools suited to the individual child so that each student is performing to the best of their ability. For example, students performing poorly during group instruction time would be provided with a facilitator, and possibly only have to join the very end or very beginning of group instruction time. Any implemented prompts would be systematically faded out by the staff to prevent prompt dependency.

<u>ABA Principle: Conceptually Systematic</u>- Conceptually systematic day programs would have interventions and curriculum rooted in science. Science and research would drive critical decisions, not opinions or staff preference. Families would be trained in empirically sound behavioral strategies and teaching methods, and staff would be careful not to espouse their own opinions and beliefs to clients as if that information were fact. Rather, staff would limit their communication and advice to families to behavioral analytic information which has been validated in research.

<u>ABA Principle: Behavior Management</u>- ALL staff would be trained in behavior management techniques. This would ensure more confident staff who are thoroughly equipped to handle mild, moderate, or severe problem behaviors, and would reduce the need to **react to,** rather than **prevent** problem behaviors. Specific procedures would be put in place to monitor staff's behavioral management effectiveness, and ongoing training would be provided on positive behavior supports that can be implemented in the day program. Consistent follow through of behavioral interventions would be required of staff (as well as the family) and staff should be trained in the use of Establishing Operations (E.O.) to know how to capture or contrive a child's motivation to promote learning.

<u>ABA Principle: Generalization & Maintenance</u>- Curriculum content should be taught in multiple environments for all children to encourage retaining of information, and so the children can apply what has been learned. Community Outings would be planned so that children can generalize skills

learned at the day program. Carry over of skills and procedures to the home environment would be built into the day program, through parent coaching or visits into the home environment. Review of previously learned skills would be embedded into the curriculum to ensure children are not regressing and to alert staff if old material needs to be re-visited. Students who tend to lose old information more quickly than others will have their instruction modified to include more maintenance tasks.

ABA Principle: Small Teacher Student Ratios- Children should receive much of their instruction in a 1:1 or small group format (less than 5 children). The ratio would be kept small until the child has grasped the concept and is demonstrating learning, after that point large group instruction (more than 5 children) can be introduced for generalization, and social purposes. Children who are not yet ready to benefit from large group instruction (e.g. Circle Time) would sit in on these activities, while being prompted to participate as much as they can. That may mean that little Nicole can only sit in Circle Time for 4 minutes at a time, and then needs to take a short break in another room.

ABA methodology can include a variety of teaching strategies, such as Discrete Trial Teaching (DTT), Natural Environment Teaching (NET), Incidental Teaching, and Task Analyses. In my opinion, a quality center or day program will include a variety of teaching modalities throughout each day so that learning occurs across multiple environments and instructors.

As children enter the day program they may need more intensive and structured instruction, such as Discrete Trial Teaching, in order to learn most efficiently. A former supervisor of mine described DTT by stating it boils teaching down to its essence, and removes distractions so the child can learn. I agree completely. For younger children or children who have not yet "learned how to learn" (child cannot attend, has no eye contact, does not respond to instructions, etc), DTT gives them the tools to learn effectively.

As the children progress through instruction and become accustomed to the clinic program and fast paced teaching, more naturalistic teaching methods can be incorporated, such as NET and Incidental Teaching. Generalization can also be incorporated, through group instruction or community outings.

Many people think of an Autism intervention center and picture staff doing DTT with children at little tables all day long. While some centers do look like that, the more variety and generalization that be incorporated into the day...the better!

PHYSICAL LAYOUT

Planning the layout or organizing of classrooms, work spaces, or instructional areas is one of my favorite parts of what I do! There are so many elements that must come together to make a learning space functional, conducive to learning, and successful. Excellent teachers already know about how the physical layout of a classroom can improve learning and reduce off task behaviors in children.

Especially when teaching children with special needs, it is so important to think about the flow of a room, noise level, colors of the wall, and the space/physical boundaries between areas. Children who already have difficulty paying attention or focusing will need a very organized and clutter free space to learn in.

The layout of the learning space also helps the teachers and staff to have a smooth, "dead spot" free day, where one activity flows seamlessly into the next, and supplies and materials are easily located. Organization is a big part of any in-home ABA program, and it's just as important in the school, or inside of a day program. It is planning and organization that cause instructional time to be most effective. Some staff will be more organized than others, as people have differing ideas of what "organized" is. It would be helpful to have a program wide system of organization, with the recommended layout for each room and area drawn out and labeled. This reduces confusion and helps staff to know what is expected of them, and what goes where. Staff wandering around searching for materials, children getting into restricted reinforcers, and teachers misplacing progress notes only reduces time that could be spent working with a child, and makes the work day feel chaotic and stressful.

Each area or room should be plainly marked and labeled, with both a word and picture label being recommended. This helps children who can and can not read identify rooms/areas, transition successfully, and be able to put away materials or toys in the correct place. Materials should be kept near, or in, the room/area they are used for. The following layout is intended to be a sample template that can be modified to fit the needs of your day program:

Small Group Instruction Tables	Large Group Instruction Area	1:1 Working Area
Cubbies, Shelves, Cabinets	Labels, Labels, Labels	Multiple Centers
Transition Areas	Functional Skill Areas	Mix of Quiet Areas & Loud Areas

-Small group instruction: This would be an area where 1 staff is working with groups of 2-4 children at a time, either individually or as all together. The children may be given individual work assignments to complete, or the teacher may be leading a group activity. A small table is suggested, where the teacher can easily provide assistance and the children are in close physical proximity. Proximity can be an issue for children with Autism, with many kiddos avoiding or refusing to sit near other children. This is a great skill to work on in a day program setting.

-Large group instruction: This would be an area where 1 or more staff members are working with groups of 4 or more children, usually all together. An example would be Circle Time, or Story Time. The children can sit on the floor in front of the teacher (with any necessary aides sitting with individual children), or the children could be seated at desks with a teacher standing in front of them. Group instruction can be very hard for a child with Autism, and it may take time and much 1:1 assistance before a child with Autism can attend and learn in a group setting. Children with special needs can benefit from space barriers, such as pillows, colored squares, or blankets to sit on in a group setting. This helps the child know where to keep their body in relation to others, and also serves as a reminder to stay seated and still. Another idea for large group instruction would be a room set up to resemble a classroom, with desks, a chalkboard, and an instructor standing at the front of the room to teach a group of children. I have only seen this in a few center facilities, but I think it's a great idea for teaching group attending. The children would be expected to sit at their desks appropriately, work independently, and raise their hand to answer questions or respond to teacher directives.

-1:1 Area: This area would be used for 1 staff to work directly with 1 child utilizing an ABA instructional format such as Natural Environment Teaching, Discrete Trial Training, or Verbal Behavior. A small table could be used, the floor, a cubicle, or even a bench. The 1:1 work areas need to be private and separated to minimize distractions. Wall partitions, shelves, or cabinets can be used to separate work areas. Children should not be placed directly next to other children who are working 1:1, near noisy hallways, or near large windows. For a child with Autism, anything can be used as a distraction. Try to minimize distractions as much as possible in the 1:1 work area, and keep this area plainly decorated.

-Cubbies/Shelves/Cabinets: Cubbies, shelves, and cabinets will be essential to keeping spaces organized and clutter free. It is recommended that toys or materials that the children can engage with be kept at the child's level (such as placed inside a cubby that sits on the floor). Teaching materials, reinforcers, etc., should be kept out of the reach of children and inside cabinets, teacher closets, or under lock and key. An exception to this would be keeping reinforcers in sight but out of reach (such as in a large clear bin that is securely locked) to encourage vocal requesting. Every item should have a place, and separating items from each other will help with organization. Large foam blocks should not be thrown into a container with small Legos. Those toys should be separated and placed into cubbies or on shelves, to help with organization and order. The children will be better able to maintain order and keep spaces clean if they know where items go. A color coding system can be helpful for children who cannot read, such as a blue shelf for books, a red shelf for DVD's, and a yellow shelf for art supplies. Then the teacher could tell the children to "put all the blocks away in the yellow bin", as she points to the bin.

-Labels, labels, labels: Labels are the best friend of organization. When teaching children with Autism, even if the child is very young it is important to help that child learn to identify objects in their environment. Labeling helps children learn to receptively identify common objects, even if the child is unable to expressively identify the object. The areas, rooms, materials, toys, and items inside the day program should be clearly labeled. Both a written and photo label is recommended. Children with Autism are often visual learners, and being able to see a photo (and not just a word) can help the child learn where things go, and also to transition better. Saying to a child "Go to the Circle Time area" may not be helpful if the child hasn't yet learned what that means. However, saying that same statement while holding up a photo of the Circle Time area is much more helpful because now the child can look for the area that matches the photo. The individual cubbies should be labeled, rooms should be labeled, and selves should be labeled. Depending on the needs of the child, more or less labels may be necessary to interact successfully with the environment. It is better to create more labels than you may need than to not have enough.

-Multiple Centers: The purpose of placing Centers, or independent play activities, in the day program is to teach children appropriate leisure activities, to help teach or generalize skills, and to teach the children to attend to an activity for a set amount of time. Many schools incorporate Centers into the day. Examples of common Centers include Computers, Art, Imaginative Play, Science, and Music. The children are taught to play in each area for a specific amount of time, and then to move into a new area. This play may be alone or with other children. For children with special needs, it is advised that you first teach the child to play in a Center alone. Once the skill has been learned and the child understands what they are supposed to do, you can add other children into the Center. It is suggested to have 2-4 Centers for very young children and 3-7 Centers for older children. Centers can be academic or non-academic, such as a Math Center or a Ball Play Center. Each Center needs to have its own distinct area, and be spaced a good distance away from another Center. You can create a sign to label each Center so that over time the child can request which Center they want to go to. Center locations do not have to be permanent. You can move them if needed, so you can keep an eye on the children. It is highly recommended that you put away the Center materials when not in use (in tubs, containers, cabinets, or just cover the Center with a curtain) so the Centers don't become distracting when they are not in use. Depending on the communication style and cognitive level of the child you want to teach them to go to a Center when told to, to stay in it for a specified amount of time, and to be appropriate with the materials inside the Center. Here is a suggestion: Get a timer and place it near the Center. Take the child to the Center and briefly go over the rules of the Center using positive language. Focus on what you what the child to do, and not on what you want them to avoid doing. So instead of saying "Don't scream in the Center", say "Remember to use an inside voice in the Center". Then point to the Center sign and say "Its time to go to Centers". Direct the child into the Center and set the timer for a short time period (e.g. 45 seconds). If the child is inappropriate, remind them how you want them to behave. If the child tries to leave the Center, immediately take them back to the Center with minimal attention or language and say "Go to (Art/Reading/Music, etc) Center". Once the timer goes off, allow the child to leave the Center and give them praise depending on how well they did. When initially teaching Centers, start with very short time increments and be sure to place highly preferred activities in the Center.

-Transition Areas: Whether the day program is a full or ½ day program, successful transitions will be a necessary part of the day to keep things running smoothly. Transitions are the time between activities, such as the time between Free Play and Circle Time or the time between washing hands and eating snack. A failure to plan for transitions will lead to loud, chaotic, confusing transitions. Children with Autism thrive in environments full of activities and structure, with minimal gaps in the schedule. It is highly recommended to avoid lots of "down time" or sitting and waiting on things to begin, when dealing with children with Autism. Transition areas can easily be added to any room or area, by placing colored tape on the floor, beanbags in the corner, or if space will not allow, playing short transition games. For example, singing songs or going through flashcards with children as they stand in line while waiting to go outside. Particularly for a child who has not learned to wait, sitting or standing around and waiting for the next activity to happen is very likely to lead to problem behaviors.

-Functional Skill Areas: Functional skills, also called adaptive skills, are skills that are necessary to have meaningful interaction with the environment and to be successful with daily living. This could include knowing how to prepare one's own meals, or being able to unpack a book bag and put items away. In a day program setting, functional skill areas can include regular living areas that are modified for the children to have access to. In the kitchen, visual supports can be added so children can prepare meals from simple (a sandwich) to complex (a pizza). A recipe box can be added (with words and pictures) so children can practice cooking skills. In the office, children can be taught to use a computer, printer, calculator, etc, to perform simple office tasks. If children have potty accidents, they can learn to wash and clean their own clothing and then clean up the area where they voided (teaching chores). These valuable adaptive skills can help the children to gain independence skills, perform chores at home, or learn vocational skills that will make them desirable employees one day.

-Mix of Quiet Areas & Loud Areas: The rooms/areas inside the day program should be organized in such a way that quiet activities and loud activities are not placed directly next to each other. This could be very distracting for a child with Autism, and could leads to inattentiveness or problem behaviors. Quiet areas could include a reading space, quiet sensory activities (such as a bean bag and white noise machine), or independent task areas. Loud areas could include loud sensory activities (such as crash pads and a ball pit), large group area, or manipulative play area. The flow from one area to the next should be mindful of what type of activity will take place in each section of the day program. Children who are noisily playing in a ball pit shouldn't have to be quiet because someone is reading a book a few feet from them. Likewise, a child is quietly sitting on a bean bag shouldn't have to be distracted by Circle Time occurring right next to them. Activities can occur in separate rooms if space will allow, or large and open rooms can be divided by shelves, partitions, cubicles, curtains, etc. What is most important is that the children have specific areas where they can be loud and active, or quiet and calm.

DAILY SCHEDULE

The daily schedule is related to the structure and organization of the day program. If you are running a day program with no daily schedule, its very likely the day is filled with behavioral outbursts from the children, "dead spots" where staff looks for materials and stands around deciding what to do next, and chaotic transitions that go on and on as staff desperately try to move the children from one area to the next. Not only is a lack of a consistent schedule stressful for staff, it's also quite stressful for the children. This isn't just an Autism issue; typically developing children crave structure and order as well. Most teachers (especially teachers of very young children) will tell you that without the structure of a schedule, the day would quickly become stressful and chaotic, and how do the children typically react to a chaotic, loud, stressful environment? With *problem behaviors.*

The day program should be more than just direct, intensive instruction. The entire day should not just be children working 1:1 with teaching staff. I have seen Centers like that, and those children didn't appear to be having much fun, shuttling between teachers all day and sitting at little tables. **Learning should be fun**. A day program should incorporate a variety of learning environments, across instructors (e.g. Ms Katie shouldn't work with David all day long. Switch it up), and include non-academic skills such as music, socializing, self help skills, dance, fine motor development, life skills, play skills, etc.

The daily schedule can be adapted to fit the needs of the day center. It might work best to have a generalized schedule that the entire program follows. Or, the children might need individual schedules that they carry with them as they move throughout the day. The schedule should contain visuals as well as words (for very young or nonverbal children, just visuals is fine), and should be clearly posted where children can see it and easily reference it. A common mistake that I see professionals make is taking the time to create a visual schedule, posting it on the wall, and expecting student behavior to change. It is very likely that you will need to teach the visual schedule to the child, maybe even repeatedly. It may not be enough to just post the schedule, if a child never looks at it, or walks right past it. A daily schedule will help the children understand what will happen in their day, what activities come next, what will **not** happen in their day (such as removing the playground icon from the schedule because it is raining), where activities will take place (which room/part of the building), etc. For example if a child keeps attempting to bolt out the door because they want to go outside, take that child to the daily schedule and say "It's not time to go outside. We go outside after lunch", and point to the schedule as you explain to the child why they cannot go outside.

In my time spent training staff, I have also noticed that daily schedules don't just benefit the children; they can benefit the staff. Staff will sometimes tell me they don't have daily schedules posted because the children don't need them or are too old for them. However, these same staff members may "lose track" of the day. They might spend too long in one activity, causing the activity after it to be cancelled. Or they might forget to gather supplies for an art activity which means now the children must sit and wait 20 minutes for art to begin. Having a schedule of what happens in each day and what times each activity must happen can also be very helpful for keeping the teaching staff organized and on a schedule. If I know that Circle Time must start in 15 minutes, then I know to begin transitioning the children, cleaning up our current activity, and setting up the Circle Time materials.

When creating a daily schedule, it's important to design it with a typical day in mind. The schedule can also be modified as needed to reflect schedule changes or activity modifications. For example, if the children go out into the community once each month for Fun Day or Field Trip, that doesn't need to go on the daily schedule. Remember you can always modify the schedule as needed, so every single change in the day that could happen does not need to go on the permanent daily schedule.

To create the daily schedule you will need to know the format of the day (it's important to be as specific as possible. "Large Manipulative Play" is preferred over "Free Time"). Decide when transitions need to happen, and how an ideal day should flow from one activity to the next. For example, passive activities could be interspersed with more active activities, and activities that take place outside could be placed back to back on the schedule rather than having teaching staff constantly shuttling children back and forth. Daily schedules can be purchased online, but I recommend just creating one since they are simple to make, and the best daily schedule needs to be individualized. I suggest using colorful paper, photos/visuals, and laminating the daily schedule so it will last longer.

Below is a sample of what a daily schedule could look like, along with explanations of each suggested activity. Feel free to modify this sample based on what would work best for your day program setting.

A visual should be placed next to each activity (for example, a photo of a plate of food to represent snack time), and clock faces could also be added to the schedule to help the children learn what time certain activities take place:

Daily Schedule

9:00 Arrival/Block Play – As children arrive to start the day, there should be a selection of activities placed out for the children to play with. This avoids children aimlessly wandering around or engaging in problem behaviors. Designate a specific area where all of the children will be (makes it easier to supervise the children) and allow them to choose from a small number of toy options. Teachers should greet all children as they arrive, and prompt children to greet each other with a wave, smile, or greeting. Be sure to check in with the parents to gather important information such as: Did the child eat breakfast? How did the child sleep last night? What time will the child be picked up?

9:30 Circle Time/Music & Movement – Circle Time for children with Developmental Disabilities should be short and sweet. 10-20 minutes is long enough. Circle Time should include a variety of academic activities and lessons such as math, phonics, songs & music, etc. I recommend visiting local schools and observing how the teachers run Circle Time and the type of content taught during Circle Time. As much as possible, the

Autism day program should help transition children into typical classrooms; therefore it can be helpful to teach the children based on what the local schools are doing. When working with children with disabilities or young children it can be helpful to start the day with energetic music, and letting the children get up and move! Incorporate into Circle Time songs that encourage clapping, shouting, jumping, marching, etc.

9:45 1:1 Table work/Natural Environment Teaching – This would be the 1:1 ABA therapy portions of the day. Depending on the methodology of the day program, this could include types of ABA such as Discrete Trial Teaching or Verbal Behavior. It is important in the day program format that children are receiving 1:1 direct instruction multiple times a day. Natural Environment Training should also be incorporated, particularly if more structured teaching methodologies are used, such as Discrete Trial Training. It is important that the children are taught at and away from the work table.

10:45 Snack/Adaptive Skills – Meal times are a great opportunity to teach skills in the natural environment, by focusing on specific skill areas such as feeding, fine motor (using utensils), hygiene (using a napkin), and social skills (encourage the children to have conversations with each other as they eat).

11:00 1:1 Table work/Natural Environment Teaching - This would be the 1:1 ABA therapy portions of the day. Therapists can work with children 1:1 on individualized programs, being sure to incorporate a variety of items/activities that the child finds reinforcing. If possible, 1:1 therapy should be conducted in individual therapy rooms. Natural Environment Training, or NET, would include more naturalistic learning that occurs across environments and materials. For example, if the child is learning to label colors then during NET time the therapist can take the child outside to collect red flowers, or green leaves. More structured ABA teaching methods, such as Discrete Trial Teaching, should also include less structured teaching time, such as Natural Environment Training.

11:45 Arts & Crafts/Sensory Exploration – Arts & Crafts time can incorporate varied sensory experiences, fine motor skills, motor coordination, and social skills if the children complete activities in a group. For younger children or lower functioning children, sensory play can often be a precursor to teaching play skills. For children with Autism who will not engage with a toy, they may be much more likely to shove their hands into a bin of rice, or happily paint their toes yellow. I suggest working with a variety of materials, such as glitter, glue, Popsicle sticks, paint, pudding, ice, confetti, silk, yarn, and much more! Be sure to alternate between structured teacher-led art activities, and placing out a few sensory options and just letting the children explore and have fun.

12:00 Chores/Prepare for Lunch/Adaptive Skills – Adding in tasks, or chores, for each child will help teach functional skills that can easily be generalized to the home environment. Children can be responsible for setting the table, handing out napkins, pouring juice, washing dishes, etc. For older children, light cooking skills can be taught such as popping a bag of popcorn for snack. Be sure to consult with the family and see if there are any particular adaptive skills they want their child to learn.

12:15 Lunch & Conversation - Meal times are a great opportunity to teach skills in the natural environment, by focusing on specific skill areas such as feeding, fine motor (using utensils), hygiene (using a napkin), and social skills (encourage the children to have conversations with each other as they eat).

12:30 1:1 Table work/Natural Environment Teaching - This would be the 1:1 ABA therapy portions of the day.

2:00 Child Directed Centers/Social Interactions – Centers are work stations focused on teaching a specific skill or targeting social interaction. A Center could be pretend play, games, water play, writing, or puzzles, just to name a few examples. The teaching staff should designate a few Center options (both fun and academic) and rotate the children through each Center. Keep the Centers small (maximum of 3 children in a Center at one time) for maximum social interaction and engagement. Encourage the children to share materials, talk to their peer, ask questions of their peer, and interact with each other in the Center. During Center time the teaching staff should be in facilitator mode, and really step back from direct prompting to more indirect prompts. This could include prompting through a peer, using visual cues, or modeling appropriate behavior for the children to imitate.

2:45 Group Storytime/ Quiet Reading – There will always be some children who do not want to participate in a group story time activity, so its ideal to have an option of letting children sit behind the group and read quietly to themselves. It may help the children to listen and attend to the book if they are allowed to sit on comfortable cushions or pillows, or to hold non-distracting items in their lap, such as a plush toy. Just like with Circle Time, place a time limit on this group activity to prevent problem behaviors from occurring due to boredom or lack of interest. Encourage group participation during the story to keep the children engaged, such as having the students all stand up and jump every time a character in the book jumps.

3:00 Departure/Large Manipulative Play - As children depart and parents arrive at the end of the day, there should be a selection of activities placed out for the children to play with. This avoids children aimlessly wandering around or engaging in problem behaviors. If a child does not select an activity to engage with, use prompting and redirection to help the child find something to do. Designate a specific area where all of the children will be (makes it easier to supervise the children) and allow them to choose from a small number of toy options. As parents leave with their children, teaching staff should be taking time with each parent to talk about the child's day: successful parts of the day, any behavioral challenges, etc. Teaching staff could also use this time to complete paperwork/collect data, clean up, or prepare materials for the next day.

CREATING OPPORTUNITIES FOR SOCIAL INTERACTION

Individuals with Autism can present with a wide variety of socialization issues and challenges. Difficulties can arise in making eye contact with others, responding to greetings from others, appropriately sitting in close proximity to others, or engaging in back and forth conversation with a peer.

Unfortunately, it isn't uncommon for me to have a client who does not have any friends. I believe everyone should have the chance to make friends and have companionship, so social skill development is often an important skill that I will target to teach. When thinking about improving social skill development it is important to realize all the separate skills that combine to make socializing with others possible. This could include: appropriate play skills, a system of communication (either vocal or nonvocal), appropriate waiting skills, minimal to no problem behaviors or repetitive, self-stimulatory behaviors, attending skills, imitation skills, and more. When professionals use the term "social skills", they are really defining a broad category of separate discrete behaviors.

What can make a center based ABA intervention program so unique from both home or school based services, is the opportunity for intensive social skill development. Social skills can be repetitively practiced, generalized upon, and embedded into a variety of activities each day and across multiple peers of varying functioning levels. The centers or facilities I have enjoyed working with the most are the ones who are able to include typically functioning peers to provide a socialization model, even if only for parts of the day. It is so helpful for children with Autism to spend time with typically developing peers. However, this isn't possible for every intervention center.

Social skills can be embedded into almost all parts of the day at a center based program, because there are multiple peers within close proximity the majority of the day. If ratios are kept low, then that makes it easier to prompt and teach interaction between peers all day long. It is much harder to work on social skills with individuals with Autism, if ratios are too high (e.g. 1 teacher and 6 children). Especially for prompting and accurate data collection to be done, ratios must be kept small.

So how can social skills be taught?

1. For younger or lower functioning children, encourage developmentally appropriate play and interaction. If the child is at the level of only being able to engage in parallel play, then encourage that. Use excited tone of voice and facial expressions to make play fun, and help the child move from stimming with objects to interacting with them. Start with simple sensory-motor play (such as digging shapes out of Jell-O) and gradually move up to playing with toys, and then with peers.

2. For older or higher functioning children, help them to understand those "hidden" social rules that many children with Autism can miss. This can include knowing when to say "I'm sorry", knowing when someone is NOT a friend but is a bully, knowing when someone is being sarcastic, reading your friends faces to know when they are bored with you, etc. Encourage play dates, or other 1:1 peer opportunities with typically developing children full of shared activities and conversation around topics both children choose (Do not let the child with Autism dominate the conversation or the play activity. This turns peers off).

3. Track progress with social skill development by creating goals based on deficits. For example, "Kelsey will be able to respond to a greeting from a peer by waving, within 2 seconds of the greeting being given". Collect data each day across a variety of social interactions to determine progress on the skill. If no progress is being made, the skill may be too difficult or the child may need more opportunities to practice.

4. Understand that most social skill goals are taught using an adult model first: This is because typically it is hard to get a child to participate for the necessary repeated trials of learning, and also children are usually less aggressive towards adults than peers. For example, the child may find it easier to learn to share with you first, than with another child. Once you have some success teaching the social skill using an adult, at that point you can introduce a peer.

Once you have success with a peer, then you can teach the social skill in a group of peers. Be careful with typical peer selection as well. You want to pick a peer who is patient and kind, as well as has some leadership qualities, so you can prompt through the peer (e.g. "Stacey, go ask Lenny to give you some Play Dough").

5. Stay true to ABA methodology: Use positive reinforcement to teach and strengthen social skills, collect and analyze data to track progress, and plan for generalization of the social skills that have been taught. For example, if you teach the child to make eye contact and say "Hello" to their teacher, you also need to teach the child to exhibit this same skill to multiple peers. Once they can do that, increase the difficulty of the skill.

6. Do not expect a child to exhibit a skill they have not learned yet: I usually explain that to parents by saying "If the behavior is inconsistent, or consistently poor, then we have to believe the child doesn't know what to do". If you know a child has poor social skills then don't be surprised if he/she hits peers during Circle Time. Expect that the child will need help being appropriate in social situations, in addition to structured and intensive ABA instruction.

7. Don't underestimate the importance of play skills, in order for children to be able to socially interact. Children with poor or no play/leisure skills tend to mouth or stim off of any object or toy you hand them, ignore toys or objects in their environment, repetitively engage with random materials such as carpet lint, pebbles, etc., or may need to be constantly kept engaged as they do not know what to do with "free time".

8. Communication is also key to social interaction. If a child is nonverbal and has no consistent method of expressing needs and wants, then how will they communicate they don't want to play? Or that a peer is being too loud or annoying? Most likely, this will be communicated through aggression (hitting peers, biting peers, etc). It is necessary to teach a consistent mode of communication (including replacing aggression with communication) to see improvement with social skill development.

9. Minimizing problem and repetitive behaviors is essential for promoting social interaction, as aggression, self-stimulatory behaviors, mouthing, etc., can all be stigmatizing. Typically

developing peers, even at a very young age, may start to avoid the child on the playground who seems a bit...different. It can be very sad to watch your client try to interact, and their peers just are not interested. It is so important as a professional to help your client learn about social stigma and relating to peers in positive ways. I tell many parents of my clients that they need to be "cheerleaders" for their child's social development in school. Be the fun family that always has kids over, that throws the best Halloween parties, and that has the coolest play dates. We want typical peers to approach, not avoid, our clients with Autism.

NEW CLIENT INTAKE PROCESS

"Intake" is the process of accepting new clients into the day program. It is important to have an intake process that is overseen by the same person every time (such as the Program Director), and is consistent each time. If children are accepted into the day program without a proper intake process this could cause many problems, such as having insufficient information on the child, being unaware of dangerous behaviors, or taking on clients when the day program is not adequately prepared to meet their needs.

The intake process should be the first step anytime a family wants their child to attend the day program. This process could take a few hours, or a few days, just depending on how much time can be dedicated to completing intakes. The parents/caregivers will need to be interviewed, relevant records should be reviewed (such as recent reports or evaluations from a pediatrician or Speech Therapist), an assessment/evaluation will need to be completed, and it may be helpful to observe the child in the home setting, as well as at the day program among other children.

The assessment process needs to include an assessment tool, such as the ABBLS-R or VB-MAPP. These assessment tools cover many important skill domains that a typically developing child would easily master. For a child with Autism, they may possess gaps in skill development that would be revealed during a thorough assessment. Depending on how many people deliver the assessment, it could take anywhere from a few hours to a few days to complete. The parents can be very helpful during the assessment process by answering questions about specific skill sets the child may currently exhibit, or skills the child once had and has now lost.

The observation process should take place during the assessment (which can happen at the day program), as well as inside the child's home. It is common that children with Autism behave very differently from one environment to the next, or around different people. Observation should focus on looking for problem behaviors, skill deficits, barriers to instruction, issues with transitioning, attending, etc. Observation can also reveal information about family functioning and interactions, which can help tailor the needs of the initial family training. For example, it may be noted during observation that the parents need help with delivering consistent consequences to their child.

During the intake process, the family should be encouraged to ask questions about the day program, staff qualifications, ABA methodology, etc. I often meet families who, even as they are requesting ABA services, really do not know what ABA is or what types of skill gains are realistic. The family should be made to feel comfortable and confident in the competency and expertise of the day program, and should get all of their questions answered and concerns addressed.

When I do intake with a new client, in addition to answering all of the family's questions and addressing concerns, I also am asking the family a multitude of questions. I need to know the family's expectations of therapy, the learning history of the child, and current concerns and challenges. All of this information is necessary for me to know how best to teach the child, and also if my expertise is suitable for the needs of the child.

I would suggest the following content be covered during the intake process:

- Diagnosis History: When was the child diagnosed? What is the official diagnosis? Does the child have multiple diagnoses?
- Demographic Information: This would include basic information such as date of birth, allergies, medications, school, etc.
- Past and Current Treatments/Therapies: Does the child receive any other therapy treatments or have they in the past? If so, how successful was the therapy? Do the parents plan on combining many therapies at once? Do the parents expect the day program to allow other therapy providers inside to work with their child?
- Goals & Expectations of Treatment: What do the parents expect out of treatment? What goals do they have for their child? What goals do they have for themselves? What type of improvement are they expecting to see, in what timeframe?

- Problem Behaviors: Are there any current behavior problems? If no, what problem behaviors occurred previously (this is an important question because old behaviors can pop back up)? How do the parents handle problem behaviors? Are these methods successful?
- Child's Current Functioning: This information will mainly come from conducting an assessment, but the parents can also be interviewed about their child's functioning across skill domains (motor skills, social skills, language skills, self-help skills, etc).
- Policies & Procedures: During the intake process, the policies and procedures of the day program need to be explained in detail to the parents, along with encouraging the parents to ask questions about how the day program is organized or set up.
- Overview of ABA/Tour of the Day Program: The parents will likely have questions about the treatment offered at the day program, and how it can help their child. The intake process is a great time to describe how skills are taught using ABA methodology and how problem behaviors are reduced. Once intake is completed, the parents can receive a tour of the day program facility and sit and observe some of the teaching staff work with children 1:1. I find the most practical way to explain ABA is to let families/parents sit and observe teaching happen.

Once a new child has started attending the center, I would advise against immediately throwing them into the mix. Take a few days to observe the child, get to know them, and let them get to know the center. This is a great time to establish rapport (pairing), conduct reinforcer preference assessments, and get the child adjusted to the routine and structure of the center. This slow fading-in process can also help lower anxiety for children who may not be used to an intervention center, and may still be dealing with some separation anxiety from leaving mom and dad.

HIRING STAFF

The direct staff members are the backbone of the day program. They are the ones who will work 1:1 with the children day after day, teaching skills and applying behavior management strategies. I highly suggest taking the time to locate and hire quality staff who are truly passionate and energetic, as excellent staff lead to an excellent program!
The finest and most expensive toys, materials, equipment, furniture, books, etc. cannot compensate for lethargic, apathetic, poorly trained, and non -motivated staff.

For intensive teaching, a 1:1 staff ratio would be best. For group instruction and more naturalistic teaching strategies, a 1:2-4 ratio may be possible, depending on the needs of the children. Some children will require 1:1 assistance, even during natural setting activities such as eating a meal.

I believe that staff can be trained on how to do their job, such as delivering reinforcement, training parents, and data collection. I don't believe that an individual with low energy and a bad attitude can necessarily be trained out of that. For that reason, I suggest seeking out staff members who enjoy working with children, are energetic and pleasant to be around, and who truly have a positive attitude about them.
Over the years, I have worked with staff who always seemed to be frustrated, annoyed, or fatigued. Everyone has bad days and good days, and even the most patient person can become frustrated by a challenging client. However, an individual who is agitated more often than they are calm should not be working with children with special needs. This field can be very trying and stressful, and these children deserve to be taught by a mature individual who is in control of their emotions, and who truly cares about the work they are doing. It is an individuals love and passion for this field that will get them through those bad days.

Characteristics I look for during the staffing/hiring process include:

- Positive attitude
- Open, warm personality

- Experience working with special needs children
- Experience working with children
- Direct ABA knowledge or experience (this would be great to find, but can be difficult to find)
- Punctual and responsible
- Mature
- Excellent self-assessment skills (sure, anyone can name their strengths.....but what are your weaknesses?)
- Organized
- Asks questions about the position and the company
- Smiles!
- Self-starter/Can take initiative
- Responds well to feedback and constructive criticism
- Looking for a career, not just a job
- Experience with setting, and meeting specific goals

As far as education, persons with Psychology, Education, Social Work, Counseling, or Sociology backgrounds can step into the world of ABA very easily. I have worked side by side with professionals from a variety of educational backgrounds, and it can be an incredible learning experience. A person with training in Nursing will bring unique knowledge to a day program that a person with Counseling training may not, and vice versa. Be open minded about educational backgrounds, and focus more on how the individual performed in school, what was their GPA, how adept are they at multi-tasking, etc. Ask to see samples of college level work, such as reports or projects, to get an idea of how the individual expresses ideas and concepts to convey a point.

As far as experience, it can be quite difficult to locate experienced ABA therapists. The demand far exceeds the supply, and many highly experienced individuals expect to be paid high salaries. A small ABA center may not be able to afford to pay staff high salaries. If possible, seek to hire staff with at least 6-12 months of ABA experience, working with children of various ages. If this cannot be located, then seek individuals with experience teaching, working with children, providing individualized and compassionate care (such as an individual who comes from a nursing background), or working with specific special needs populations (such as ADHD or Autism).

Any new staff will require initial training, and then continuous OTJ (on the job) training. Even an individual with years of experience will need to learn how things are done at the center, and get to know each individual client and their history of learning. I recommend having all new staff participate in at least 20 hours of ABA and Autism specific training.

As part of the interview process I recommend giving a tour of the day program, and allowing interviewees to briefly observe current staff. When I have interviewed for ABA positions, I have found such direct observations to be a valuable way to determine if the work setting and culture is right for me. This can also be a great time to ask questions of current staff members, and get questions answered. I would also encourage allowing current staff members to participate in staff interviews, as very often the business owner or management is the only one interacting with incoming staff. However, the teaching staff typically know much more about the day to day functioning of the day program, as well as what personalities will mesh well with the current team.

I definitely believe that beyond education and experience, any new staff must be a *good fit* within the company culture. Someone might have excellent references and years of experience, but maybe they are too introverted and reserved to fit in very well with current staff. This could create an uncomfortable situation for the current staff, as well as for the new hire. In my opinion, goodness of fit is just as important as checking credentials and experience.

EVALUATING & REPORTING PROGRESS

There are many day programs without a consistent and valid way of measuring progress, and the result of that is programming that tends to be one size fits all (also known as "cookie cutter"), and isn't individualized to what each student really needs. When teaching children with Autism, once size fits all just is not possible. These children are far too different and unique to be lumped together.

ABA is such a widely used and respected treatment because of that last "A": Analysis. Which means, data, data, data. ABA professionals collect data on everything in order to be able to have fluid programming and treatment that is sensitive to the changing needs of the client.

In a day program, data collection and graphing data needs to be taught to all teaching staff and a priority on accurate data collection and measurement must be placed. When staff get busy, overwhelmed, or stressed, a result is often poorly collected data, or skipping data collection completely. This must be prevented by management, and staff must be supported in order to keep this from happening. There are all kinds of electronic data collection systems today that didn't exist when I first started in this field, or the families I worked for couldn't afford such systems. Invest in quality data collection tools that will help with speed, ease of use, and accuracy. There is nothing wrong with paper and pen data collection, but for newer staff it can often be much simpler to enter data directly into a laptop or to video record sessions and then graph data afterwards. I have also seen facilities where direct instruction occurs in a 2:1 ratio, so one instructor can teach and the other can collect the data. It just depends on what works best for the clinic, and what systems can be implemented to maintain quality and accurate data collection.

Data is so important in any ABA program because it tells us:

- How each child is progressing, and their individual rate of learning (rate= speed over time)
- Learning deficits or struggles, and where specifically these learning deficits occur (e.g. child is very weak in reading skills)

- Learner strengths, skills the child is very strong in (e.g. child excels at math tasks), strengths can also provide insight into the child's interests and likes
- Foundational skills that may be missing (often called pre-requisite skills), gaps in the child's learning profile
- Important skills to teach next, future programming ideas

Data collection can occur for any behavior. There is trial by trial data, first trial data (or Cold Probes), anecdotal or observational data, partial interval data, whole interval data, frequency data, etc. Data collection isn't just limited to 1:1 instructional time. Data can (and should) be collected on problem behaviors, social/peer interactions, or group attending skills. The benefit of taking data across the entire day is that specific goals can be incorporated into all activities. For example, during lunchtime the teaching staff can target multiple goals for multiple students: Christina is working on using a spoon, Cedric is working on eye contact when talking to peers, and John is working on staying seated at the table until everyone is finished eating.

Data collection can get very complicated, but it does not have to be. Particularly for natural environment teaching times, I recommend using simple checklists or forms for the teaching staff where they can mark a tally, indicate Yes or No, or circle a number from 1-5 on a rating scale. Ease and speed of use will help staff complete data more consistently, than if they are expected to complete complicated and lengthy data while simultaneously supervising children, prompting children, and maintaining safety. Be sure to provide clipboards and timers/ clickers to staff for easily collecting data on the go. The use of timers or clickers (instead of watches or mentally keeping track), along with a clipboard can sometimes make all the difference.

The selected data collection system will be determined by the goal of intervention. If the goal of intervention is to increase the amount of time the child can sit with the group for Circle Time, then duration data should be collected. If the goal of intervention is to reduce the number of times the child throws their spoon to the floor during Snack Time, then frequency data should be collected. Part of staff training should include an understanding of data collection, as well as giving staff the opportunity to practice collecting data "on the go". Multi-tasking is just part of this job! It is important that staff understand that they will be expected to observe the child, reinforce appropriate behaviors, teach a lesson, and simultaneously collect accurate data. Data can also be modified to make it simpler for staff to collect throughout their day.

Two things I would caution with data collection are:
- Is the data collection accurate for what is being measured?
- Is ALL of the data collection necessary?

These two issues are often interrelated. I find that particularly with new staff, they often do not understand why they are collecting data. This can sometimes lead to inaccurate data being collected. That may mean that to track the frequency of a behavior, staff is collecting pages and pages of ABC data. Well, if the frequency is the priority then writing a detailed description of each occurrence of behavior is unnecessary, and it wastes time. That is time where the staff could be engaged with the child. It's also important to consider if staff is taking copious amounts of data, even for good reasons, what impact does that have on the services they provide?

I have worked with newer staff who want to update me on everything that happened during the session. That sounds good on the surface, but again, it pulls time and focus away from the child. That abundant amount of data may not be necessary and there are better ways to relay that information, such as video recording the session. I want my staff to strike a balance between engaging with the child and collecting valuable data, and I recommend you do the same with your staff.

COMMUNITY BASED INSTRUCTION

One of my favorite things to do with a client is community outings. Think of these as a way to generalize what is taught at the table to a real life setting. A popular critique of ABA is that due to the structured nature (1:1, table setting) children become "robotic", meaning they will learn a skill but not actually display the skill unless asked in a specific way, by a specific person. This lack of generalization can sometimes be an issue, but if the ABA program your child or client is in teaches for generalization then this shouldn't be a concern. Generalization can be directly incorporated into instruction by varying stimuli, mixing new and mastered targets during instruction time, teaching in different locations, rotating the child among different instructors or staff, and by incorporating Community Instruction. It is not enough to teach a skill to mastery, and then move on. What will happen is as the child progresses through their programs, older skills will be forgotten. A successful and well run ABA program always plans for ways to generalize skills the child is learning.

Another reason why I enjoy working for center based facilities, is the focus on community based instruction. Centers and facilities often take the children out into the community to work on skills or generalize known skills, or center based programs can embed functional, or daily living skills, into a variety of activities. I have worked for centers that taught the children to do laundry, set a table, complete chores, mail a letter, use a computer, etc. These are all important life skills.

I must mention vocational skills, or job preparedness skills. Many classrooms begin to work on these skills when children with Autism enter into high school. However, I like to begin teaching vocational tasks as early as possible, and just build upon it as the child's functioning improves. One particular program I often teach, even to very young children, targets the ability to independently complete a variety of tasks. The child is given multiple tasks to complete for a set period of time (such as 2 minutes). The child must navigate through the tasks, completing each one in order, and then put all materials away when the timer goes off. For a young child, the activities may include beading string, matching cards, or sorting. For an older child, the activities may include sorting silverware into cups, sequencing objects, or homework/academic activities.

Most of my work experience has been as a home based therapist, so I get lots of face to face time with parents of individuals with Autism. A common lament that I hear over and over is that the family can't take the individual with Autism out into the community. Due to wandering off behaviors, aggressive behaviors, self-stimulatory behaviors, stealing behaviors, sexual behaviors (such as public masturbation), or other issues, the family feels forced to stay in the home. I feel I can state with confidence that many families would LOVE if their child's center based intervention program included opportunities for community based instruction.

Especially for older individuals, going out into the community to visit the park, grocery store, post office, or a shopping mall, is a wonderful teaching opportunity. I also find that in rural or international locations, people in the community need to develop some sensitivity towards individuals with disabilities. It is helpful for both the client and the community if your clients are out and about, being successful in public settings and participating as much as they can (depending on ability level). For one client that may mean they can go into the post office and independently mail a letter. For another client that may mean they can grocery shop at a known store, with a staff member walking directly beside them.

Community Outings also may be necessary with certain clients if they consistently act out in specific places, such as restaurants. The center can select community instruction locations based on the concerns of the families, and the needs of the children/individuals being served. Individual goals can be selected for each child, and ratios can be kept low (1:1 is recommended) so that safety is maintained. Being appropriate in public, speaking at a proper volume, staying near an adult, etc., are all important social skills. So in addition to generalization, familiarity with the community, direct instruction for specific goals, community instruction can also teach social skill development. What can't community based instruction do?! ☺

I personally enjoy spending time with the kiddos I work with in public settings and taking them to various places in the community. These children need to learn how to successfully navigate different public settings, street safety, how to be appropriate in crowds, how to interact with unknown adults, etc., and the younger you can start teaching these important life skills, the better for the child. What the staff intensively teaches at the center is very important, but it is also important that these children/individuals can be appropriate in public as well.

Examples of Community Instruction Goals:

1. Staying close to staff/parents
2. Having calm hands in public settings (not grabbing at objects or people)
3. Behavior reduction in public settings
4. Communicating with unknown peers or adults
5. Waiting, particularly waiting in line
6. Eating in public settings
7. Using public bathrooms
8. Riding in the car
9. Street safety (crossing the street, recognizing street signs, staying on the sidewalk, etc.)
10. Using a grocery list

Examples of Community Outing Activities:

1. Skill: Math/Money. Go to the store and buy something that costs $1. At the register, give the child enough change to equal $1 (such as four quarters) and have them count it out to the cashier.
2. Skill: Social Skill/Greetings. Go to Wal Mart (or any store with greeters). Explain your situation to the greeter there and ask if your child can help greet customers. If necessary, prompt the child to make eye contact and wave in addition to saying "Hello".
3. Skill: Community Signs. If the child is verbal, go for a walk and have them identify various signs in the community by name. If the child is nonverbal, go for a walk and bring a few pictures of community signs

with you. When you see a sign, stop and have the child point to the picture that matches the sign in front of them.

4. Skill: Gross Motor Skills. Take the child to a park or sensory play center. Have the child run, skip, climb, bend, squat, gallop, etc., depending on the specific skills you are targeting.

5. Skill: Eating Skills/ Self Help. Take the child to a restaurant and order some food. If you are targeting using a straw, order them a drink. If you are targeting using a knife, order them something that can be cut. Prompt the child to keep their area clean while eating, and use napkins as needed.

6. Skill: Waiting Appropriately/Transitions. Go to a place or setting that the child really loves, such as a favorite toy store. Tell the child before you go in the store that you are going in for 2 minutes only (bring a timer if necessary). Enter the store, and give the child transition warnings that you will be leaving soon, such as "We are leaving in 1 minute". Once 2 minutes has passed, tell the child it is time to go, and leave the store.

CLINICAL COORDINATION OF TREATMENT

Many times when I am working with a family their child is involved in multiple therapies. It's rare for me to have a client who receives ABA therapy, and doesn't also participate in speech therapy, occupational therapy, physical therapy, etc. Not to mention the many teachers and paraprofessionals at school the child comes into contact with everyday. I typically refer to this group of professionals, doctors, psychologists, educators, etc. as the **Treatment Team**. Everyone on the team has something to contribute that can help you when working with the client.

Some ABA center based facilities have multi-disciplinary staff. I think that's great! That makes coordinating treatment so much easier, and benefits the child. However, not every center will have a speech therapist or a nutritionist right down the hall.

Sometimes as an ABA professional you will get the opportunity to meet and connect with the various professionals in your client's life, and sometimes you won't. It is always beneficial to know the child's strengths/weaknesses across professionals, and to coordinate treatment goals.

For example, if I am targeting replacing aggression with manding then I can share that treatment goal with the speech therapist. If the speech therapist is targeting attending to a board game or other activity, then he can share that treatment goal with me. Together, we can discuss ways to incorporate each others strategies into our therapy sessions, in order to benefit the client. I don't recommend operating within a bubble, and never having any discussions or meetings with the other relevant people in the child's life. Those other professionals have valuable information to share, and the child may perform much worse or much better for them than for you. That is definitely something you would want to know. Families also like to see the various professionals helping their child interact and share information with one another.

It doesn't have to be a daunting task to coordinate clinical treatment. If face to face meetings cannot occur, then emails, telephone conferences, or progress reports can be used. A simple strategy I often implement is a communication log (seek parent consent first). At the start of the day, a simple spiral notebook is placed into the child's backpack. The teacher records updates into the notebook, the school OT and ST do the same, and then afterschool I record updates into the notebook as well. Everyone, including the parents, is able to not only share successes and setbacks the child is experiencing but also can read what the other professionals are doing. I find this is a great way to keep everybody "in the loop" despite differing schedules and availability.

When I meet with other professionals who work with my clients, they often ask me tons of questions about behavior: *How do I get the child to sit and attend? How often should I reinforce? Is the child this aggressive at home? Does the child respond to directions with you? How do I redirect the child away from repetitive self-stimulatory behaviors?*

Below are some examples of the type of information I typically share with other professionals to help them when working with my clients. I suggest these tips as a starting point when beginning clinical case coordination.

1. **Understand the ABC's of behavior**. This is your "detective tool kit" to methodically locate the function of any behavior. A=antecedent, B=behavior, and C=consequence. The antecedent means "what happened before the behavior", and the consequence means "what happened after the behavior". For example, if every time you arrive at the house to begin a session (antecedent), the child begins to cry and run away from you (behavior), and you then spend several minutes chasing the child through the house to have them begin working (consequence), then it is very likely the function of the behavior is escape from demand. To correct the behavior, you would find a new behavior that serves the same purpose. Such as teaching the child to communicate that they need a short break before beginning work.

2. **Learn what incompatible behaviors are, and use them**. An incompatible behavior is simply a behavior that the child cannot do at the same time as the target behavior. For example, if you are working with a child at a table and the child knocks the materials

onto the floor a simple incompatible behavior is to say to the child "Hands Down" or "Fold Hands" before you place anything on the table. If their hands are busy they have no opportunity to knock things onto the floor.

3. **Consistency!** Being inconsistent in your reactions to the child's behaviors is equivalent to intermittent reinforcement. By "sometimes" being firm, and "sometimes" letting things go, you are intermittently reinforcing the behavior which will cause it to increase. Decide what behaviors are unacceptable and have the same reaction every single time.

4. **Understand reinforcement**. Reinforcement is a way to increase behaviors you want to see again. If the child does something appropriate, give them a smile, hug, high five, tickle, etc. Reinforcement is a powerful way to shape behavior and also has the added benefit of making the child more interested in spending time with you. Over time you will become reinforcing to the child because in the past you have delivered reinforcement.

5. **Always finish out a demand**. Do not give any demand to the child that you are not prepared to prompt them through if necessary. If the child is across the room playing don't call out to them "Come sit down" unless you are willing to go and get them if they do not comply. A mistake I see often is a therapist arrives at a child's home and the child is tired or in a bad mood. The therapist then says to the parent "He/she doesn't want to work today, so I'm going to leave because the session would just be a bust". The next time that therapist shows up at the house, the child will just repeat the behavior to get them to leave again. Don't back down from demands or let a child escape from a demand.

6. **Fill the child's time with activities**. Children with Autism don't need much down time. In a typical session, I use all of the hours for engagement or instruction, even play breaks. ABA is intended to be intensive, and that means I need to use my time with my clients wisely. If the child has too much down time this can lead to boredom or distraction which can lead to problem behaviors. Keep the child busy and engaged with you so they don't have the opportunity to exhibit behaviors such as throwing things, crying, elopement, etc.

Along with the related professionals that you may get the opportunity to coordinate treatment across, the parents are also a part of the Treatment Team. The parents of the clients you serve have extremely valuable information to share about the child's strengths and weaknesses, the child's developmental history, what is motivating or reinforcing to the child, and much more. A small downside to working at a center based facility vs. in the home is not as much face time with the parents. However, there is a simple solution for that. Active and consistent parental involvement can still occur even if the child receives therapy outside of the home. I require all of my clients agree to a parent participation policy, and I recommend implementing one at your center or day program as well.

As a professional I rely on the parents to give me feedback about progress, to alert me of any changes in behavior, and to provide me with valuable information about their child's learning style. The magnitude of what I can accomplish as a professional is limited if the parents are not on board.

It is important to communicate to the parents during the intake process that they will be viewed as a team member. That means they will be updated on program progress, expected to collect data, expected to attend team meetings, and will receive ongoing training on ABA teaching strategies. If the parents are not involved in their child's therapy the likelihood of success is much lower. When parents are involved in the development and implementation of interventions the intervention procedures are more likely to be generalized across contexts and people, and the child is likely to learn and use skills more quickly.

ABA professionals often possess knowledge that parents do not have. This could be knowledge of behavior theory, learning strategies, or motivation and attention. It is part of my job to educate parents about every aspect of their child's programming as well as how to address behaviors, and how to make ABA a way of life in their home. This is my favorite part of my job. I love parents who ask questions and provide me with new perspectives on problem solving.

Unfortunately, some staff feel they don't have to provide parent education as part of their job. Maybe they are uncomfortable giving advice, or think parent education is only for the supervisory/management staff. However, <u>everyone</u> who works with the child has a responsibility to share information and progress with the parents, including training parents on the treatment plan strategies. The family and the ABA professionals are a team and the more we all work together the better it is for the client.

For the staff who will work at the center, I recommend stressing the importance of using every opportunity to show the family what ABA is, and how it can benefit the child. Parent education should be such an integral part of an ABA Therapist's job that if the staff called out sick the parent of the child could step in and teach the programs. For the most part parents genuinely WANT to learn strategies and techniques, and if someone would take the time to explain it to them they would be very grateful.

For the parents who will utilize the center or day program for their children, I recommend stressing a level of comfort. The parents should feel comfortable observing the staff, asking questions about the treatment plan, requesting private meetings with the Director, etc. The parents need to be able to feel confident about the services their child is receiving, and to develop a level of trust with the program staff. Trust will lead to involvement, if it occurs in a natural manner.

A very common question I get asked by new staff is "How do I get resistant or uncooperative parents to participate in parent training?"

First, it's important to look at the parents you work with using the correct set of eyes. Take off the judgmental or critical eyes, and put on compassionate eyes:

It is very hard to let someone into your home who will tell you everything you are doing wrong. It is very hard to trust a stranger to help your child. It is very hard to accept a diagnosis of Autism weeks, months, and even years after the fact. It is very hard to step out of paralyzing fear to seek help. It is very hard to admit that as a parent, you don't know what to do with your own child.

Understand that behind the verbal insults, rude demeanor, critical attitude, and apathy a parent displays towards you, could be something much more simple: <u>Fear.</u>

Every client you have will not be interested in receiving parent training. That's just reality. It is part of our job as ABA professionals to explain to a family why their involvement is so critical, and why we need their input.

I have worked with several families who were either uncooperative with treatment, or sometimes actively worked against me, and there are a few tips I have learned to help the situation. I recommend sharing these tips with staff during initial staff training, in order to proactively give them the tools they need to get resistant parents on board with treatment:

- o Start your relationship with parents off on the right foot. State from the beginning your expectations of their involvement (I suggest a parent involvement policy), and make it clear that the success of the therapy will suffer if they aren't generalizing what you are teaching.
- o Always be mindful of how you are speaking to the parents. Be aware of your tone, your demeanor, and your attitude. No parent will want to cooperate with a professional who makes them feel stupid, lazy, or like a bad parent. We aren't here to judge parents; we're here to help them.
- o Give the parents specific feedback, not general disapproval. Tell them what you want them to DO, not what you wish they would stop doing. Use action statements.
- o Require that the parents be in the home during the sessions. It's very easy for a family to view you as a babysitter if they use your session time to go grocery shopping, or get their car washed. Tell the parents that they need to be home during your sessions so they can observe and learn.
- o Don't get too involved or too close to parents. When boundaries are crossed and the parents become "your friends" it can be difficult to maintain your professional authority. If a parent views you as their buddy they may start treating your therapy recommendations as *optional*.

- o Siblings of your client are only allowed to be present during the therapy session if you are using them for a social skill program, or for peer modeling. Again: do not get trapped in the "babysitter" zone. You are a professional providing therapy and you shouldn't have to run a session while simultaneously entertaining the parents' other children.
- o Be consistent in your behavior towards the parents. Call the parents when you say you will, be on time for work, etc. Acting inconsistently towards them will cause them to distrust you, and at that point they won't be interested in listening to anything you have to say.
- o Ask open ended questions. Don't ask the parents questions that they can quickly say "Yes" or "No" to, because you won't get much information from that. Instead of asking "Are you following the 3-step prompting procedure?" say "Give me an example from this week of when you needed to use the 3-step prompting procedure."

Here are some common barriers to effective parent involvement that I have experienced when working in homes. This information can be useful to share with staff, to prepare them for the resistance they may encounter. I recommend reviewing these barriers during training and having the staff engage in various role playing scenarios to proactive ways of overcoming these barriers.

Barriers to Parent Involvement (Parent Barriers)
- "This is too much change"
- "I cant do what you do, I'm not a professional"
- "We do follow the behavior plan...sometimes"
- "The last supervisor/ABA staff member/company told me to do it this way...."
- "That wont work with my child"
- "I don't want my child to cry/be upset/dislike me"

Barriers to Parent Involvement (Staff Barriers)
- "I don't know how to get parents to participate"
- "I don't want the mom/dad to be upset with me" or "I'm uncomfortable telling the parents what to do"
- "The parents just don't listen to me"
- "I know the parents aren't involved, but lets just keep being patient with them"

There are multiple ways to respond to any of these barriers, but I will list a few below. Don't view barriers to parental involvement as mountains blocking the path, view them as doors. Once the door is opened through trust and communication, then it's a simple matter to walk through and start interacting with the parent as a team member.

Barriers to Parent Involvement (Parent Barriers)
- "This is too much change" - *The parents sought therapy in the first place because they wanted change: change in behaviors, change in skills, etc. In order to reach the goals the parent stated they wanted, change is necessary. If what the parents had tried before you was working, then you wouldn't be working with that client.*
- "I can't do what you do, I'm not a professional" - *Our job is to help show the parents how to learn ABA, and to give them the support they need to handle behavior. We don't expect them to be a professional; we expect them to be mom and dad. WE are the professionals, and we are happy to help them learn.*
- "We do follow the behavior plan...sometimes" – *For parents to reach the goals they said they wanted when therapy started, consistency is key. Would the parent be ok with you showing up to work half a session? With you only working half the week? Then why would we expect any less consistency from them?*
- "The last supervisor/ABA staff member/company told me to do it this way...." – *You can't speak for other people or other companies. They likely had their own reasons for the suggestions they gave. You can only speak for yourself. Sympathize with how confusing this must be, but politely explain that you are not that person.*

- "That won't work with my child" – *ABA is about data based decision making, not opinions or feelings. Ask the parents if they want to modify or change the program or are they willing to try it for 1-2 weeks, see what the data says, and then make a decision. Explain that we are constantly reviewing the data, and if something isn't working then it gets modified.*
- "I don't want my child to cry/be upset/dislike me" – *What if the child wanted to drink nail polish remover? Or wanted to skip school every day for a week? Or doesn't want to wear clothes outside? Would you let these behaviors happen to keep the child from crying? Sometimes we have to maintain boundaries for safety or for optimal learning that may cause children to be upset with us. They need to learn that life isn't always about what they want to do.*

Barriers to Parent Involvement (Staff Barriers)

- "I don't know how to get parents to participate" – **Yes you do**. *As ABA therapists you are agents of behavior change. You are equipped to use prompting, reinforcement, redirection, and other ABA strategies to increase appropriate behaviors in the parents, and decrease inappropriate behaviors.*
- "I don't want the mom/dad to be upset with me" or "I'm uncomfortable telling the parents what to do" – *Firstly, you are not barking orders and telling parents what to do. You are involving them in the therapy process as a team member. Your comfort level will increase as your experience and confidence increases. Part of your job is to have the tough conversations. It doesn't help the family or your client if you keep your mouth shut and allow them to reinforce problem behaviors or undermine the effectiveness of treatment. That just makes your job harder. Parents can read your discomfort and it may come off as you being inadequate or weak. This will lead right into.......*
- "The parents just don't listen to me" – *The parents may not be listening to you because you seem insecure and lack confidence. Your supervisor will explain to you the treatment plan, behavior plan, and skill goals. You are qualified and equipped to teach the*

parents what to do, provide reinforcement when they listen, and a consequence when they don't. If you carry yourself with confidence, people will listen to you.

- "I know the parents aren't involved, but lets just keep being patient with them" – *This is inconsiderate of all the people on the waiting list who are waiting to receive services, or all the other clients we could be helping and putting our time and energy into. It does not help parents or the client, to allow non-involvement to happen. That is confusing for the child, because there is one set of expectations during therapy and a completely different set outside of therapy. It doesn't help the parents, because it tells them that their passiveness is okay.*

BIBLIOGRAPHY

Ayres, A.J. (1974). The developmental of sensory integrative theory and practice. Dubuque, IA: Kendall/Hunt.

Ayres, A.J. (2005). Sensory Integration and the Child: Understanding hidden sensory challenges. 25th Anniversary Edition. Los Angeles: CA: Western Psychological Services.

Baer, D. M., Wolf, M. M., & Risley, T. R. (1968). Some current dimensions of applied behavior analysis. Journal of Applied Behavior Analysis, 1, 91–97.Ayres, A. J. (1972).

Charlop-Christy, M. H., & Carpenter, M. H. (2000). Modified incidental teaching sessions: A procedure for parents to increase spontaneous speech in their children with autism. Journal of Positive Behavior Interventions, 2, 98–112.

Charlop-Christy, M. H., LeBlanc, L. A., & Carpenter, M. H. (1999). Naturalistic Teaching Strategies (NaTS) to teach speech to Children with Autism: Historical perspective, development, and current practice. California School Psychologist, 4, 30–46.

Connor, M. (1998) A review of behavioural early intervention programmes for children with autism. Educational Psychology in Practice, 14 (2), 109–117.

Cooper, J. O., Heron, T. E., & Heward, W. L. (2007). Applied behavior analysis (2nd ed.). Upper Saddle River, NJ: Pearson.

Cummings, A. R. (1999). How much discrete trial vs. natural language training is appropriate for teaching language to children with autism. In P. M. Ghezzi, W. L. Williams, & J. E. Carr (Eds.), Autism: Behavior analytic approaches. Reno, NV: Context Press.

Cuvo, A. J. and Klatt, K. P. (1992), Effects of community-based, videotape, and flash card instruction of community-referenced sight words on students with mental retardation. Jnl of Applied Behav Analysis, 25: 499–512.

Dawson, G. & Osterling, J. (1997) Early intervention in autism. In The Effectiveness of Early Intervention (ed. M. J.Guralnick), pp. 307–324. Baltimore, MD: Paul H Brookes.

Derby, K. M., Wacker, D. P., Sasso, G., Steege, M., Northup, J., Cigrand, K., et al. (1992). Brief functional assessment techniques to evaluate aberrant behavior in an outpatient setting: A summary of 79 cases. Journal of Applied Behavior Analysis, 25, 197–209.

Dillenburger, K., Keenan, M., Gallagher, S., & McElhinney, M. (2002). Autism: Intervention and parental empowerment. Child Care in Practice, 8(3), 216-219.

Dillenburger, K., Keenan, M., Gallagher, S., & McElhinney, M. (2004). Parent education and home-based behaviour analytic intervention: An examination of parents' perceptions of outcome. Journal of Intellectual & Developmental Disability, 29(2), 119-130.

Doke, L. A., & Risley, T. R. (1972). The organization of day care environments: Required versus optional activities. Journal of Applied Behavior Analysis, 5, 453–454.

Eikeseth, S., Gale, C., Hayward, D., Morgan, S. (2009) Assessing progress during treatment for young children with autism receiving intensive behavioral interventions. Autism, 13(6), 613-633

Fenske, E. C., Zalenski, S., Krantz, P. J., McClannahan, L. E. (1985). Age at intervention and treatment outcome for autistic children in a comprehensive intervention program. Analysis and Intervention in Developmental Disabilities, 5, 49–58.

Green, G. (1996) Early behavioral intervention for autism: what does research tell us? In Behavioral Intervention for Young Children with Autism: A Manual for Parents and Professionals (eds C.Maurice & G.Green), pp. 29–44. Austin, TX: PRO-ED.

Green, G. (1996) Evaluating claims about treatments for autism. In Behavioral Intervention for Young Children with Autism: a Manual for Parents and Professionals (eds C.Maurice & G.Green), pp. 15–43. Austin, TX: PRO-ED.

Halle, J. W. (1987). Teaching language in the natural environment: An analysis of spontaneity. Journal of the Association for Persons with Severe Handicaps, 12, 28–37.

Halle, J. W., Alpert, C. L., & Anderson, S. R.(1984). Natural environment language assessment and intervention with severely impaired preschoolers. Topics in Early Childhood Special Education, 4, 36–56.

Harris, S. L. (1998) Behavioural and educational approaches to the pervasive developmental disorders. In Autism and Pervasive Developmental Disorders. Cambridge monographs in child and adolescent psychiatry (ed. F. R.Volkmar), pp. 195–208. New York: Cambridge University Press.

Landa RJ, Holman KC, Garret-Mayer E. Social and communication development in toddlers with early and later diagnosis of autism spectrum disorders. Arch Gen Psychiatry. 2007;64(7): 853–864

Mabry, J.B. (1998). Pedagogical Variations in Service-Learning and Student Outcomes: How Time, Contact, and Reflection Matter, Michigan Journal of Community Service Learning, 5(34).

McClannahan, L., & Krantz, P. (1999). Activity schedules for children with autism. Bethesda, MD: Woodbine House.

Pierce, W. D., & Epling, W. F. (1980). What happened to analysis in applied behavior analysis? The Behavior Analyst, 3, 1–9.

Rogers, S. J. (1998a) Empirically supported comprehensive treatments for young children with autism. Journal of Clinical Child Psychology, 27 (2), 168–179.

Sundberg, M. L. & Partington, J. W. (1999). The need for both DTT and NET language training for children with autism. In P. M. Ghezzi, W. L. Williams, & J. E. Carr (Eds.), Autism: Behavior analytic approaches. Reno, NV: Context Press.

Sussman, F. (1999) More Than Words: Helping Parents Promote Communication Social Skills in Children with Autism Spectrum Disorder. Toronto: Hanen Centre.

Strain, P. S. (1983). Generalization of autistic children's social behavior change: Effects of developmentally integrated and segregated settings. Analysis and Intervention in Developmental Disabilities, 3, 23–34.

Symon, J. B. (2001) Parent education for autism: issues in providing services at a distance. Journal of Positive Behavior Interventions, 3 (3), 160–174.

APPENDIX

Here are sample resources that include forms, programs, or protocols, that can be used as a template to create individualized documents for your center or facility.

Creating the Program Book:

The program book is an essential part of any ABA program. The programs tell you what skills to teach, and the programs, along with other essential documents, are all compiled inside of the program book. The program book will remain a source of information, progress, goals, and data, through the duration of the therapeutic process. Many people may view or have regular access to the program book including all of the direct therapists, the Consultant, school staff, and the parents of the client. Depending on the funding source, the information inside of the program book may be considered legal documents. For example, the data sheets can be used as record during the process IEP, or submitted to insurance companies to receive reimbursement. It is important to keep the program book neat, organized, and factual.

To create a program book you will need:
Large 3-5 in. Binder
Notebook paper
Dividers with multicolored tabs
Pencil pouch containing pens, pencils, highlighters, hand sanitizer, paperclips, timer, calculator
Transparent sheet protectors (3 hole punched)
3 hole punched manila folders

Putting the Program Book Together:
Preference Assessment, ABBLS or VB-MAPP Assessments/Checklists
Current Behavior Plan or Protocols

Daily Session Notes
Data Sheets
Manding/ NET Data Sheets
Active Programs divided by domain (Attending/Compliance, Mands, Tacts,
Listener Responding, Visual Perceptual, Play Skills, Social Behavior,
Imitation, Self Help Skills)
Mastered Programs
Parent Training/Participation Documentation

Sample Daily Data Sheet:

Date: _____   Initials: _____
*Mark "P" for Prompted, "U" for Unprompted

<u>Arrival</u>
Puts Away Backpack & Lunchbox   _____
Finds Seat   _____
Sits/Stands/Sings Appropriately during Circle Time   _____
Line-up   _____
Finds Seat   _____
Requests Reinforcer   _____
Comments_____

_____

_____

_____

<u>Lesson Time</u>
Retrieves Materials   _____   _____   _____   _____
Requests Materials   _____   _____   _____   _____
Answers 4 Questions   _____   _____   _____   _____
Completes Seatwork   _____   _____   _____   _____
Notifies of Completion   _____   _____   _____   _____
Stores Materials   _____   _____   _____   _____
Requests Reinforcer   _____   _____   _____   _____
Comments_____

_____

_____

_____

<u>Snack and Lunch</u>
Requests Getting Lunchbox   _____   _____
Requests hand washing after eating   _____   _____
Cleans station   _____   _____
Requests bathroom break after cleaning   _____   _____

Finds seat and requests Reinforcer　　_____　_____
Comments_____

_____

_____

_____

Cooperative Play

Asks what the activity will be　　_____　_____
Addresses friends to play　　_____　_____
Plays appropriately with toy　　_____　_____
Requests toy item from each friend　_____　_____
Participates in clean up　　_____　_____
Thanks friends for playing　　_____　_____
Comments_____

_____

_____

_____

Pack-Up & Pick-Up

Requests packing up Lunchbox and Backpack　_____
Retrieves items, packs up and sits　_____
Requests Reinforcer　_____
Requests change of Reinforcers　_____
Remains seated until Pick-Up　_____
Comments_____

_____

_____

_____

Sample Staff Training for the Pairing/Rapport Building Process:

PAIRING FEEDBACK FORM

Staff Name: _____   Client Name: _____

Date: _____   Setting: _____

Time: _____

Goal: To increase the frequency and quality of engagement with the client during the pairing process.

Data Method: Time Sampling

- = No Engagement   + = Engagement

1	2	3	4	5
6	7	8	9	10
11	12	13	14	15
16	17	18	19	20
21	22	23	24	25
26	27	28	29	30
31	32	33	34	35
36	37	38	39	40
41	42	43	44	45
46	47	48	49	50
51	52	53	54	55

56	57	58	59	60

Total Time Blocks Spent Engaged/Total Opportunities for Engagement:

_____/_____

Sample NET Data Sheet:

Directions: Record the frequency of each verbal operant during all NET activities. Be sure to rotate through operants for a varied NET experience. Place a (+) for an independent response and a (-) for a prompted response.

Child Name: _____

Mands	Tacts	Intraverbals	Receptive	Motor Im.	Echoics

Time: _____   Date: _____   Therapist Initial: _____

Describe Activities:

_____

_____

_____

Sample Staff Competency Checklist:

<u>SKILL COMPETENTCY CHECKLIST</u>

Month & Year: _____

Staff Name: _____

Client Name: _____

Supervision Hours Per Month: _____

Met Competency	Did Not Meet Competency	Content Area
		Proper Program Implementation
		Professional Appearance
		Response to Feedback
		Proper Tone
		Proper Reinforcement Delivery
		Consistently Arrives on Time, Adheres to Therapy Schedule
		Seeks Supervision Appropriately
		Communicates Effectively with Family
		Correct Implementation of Behavioral Interventions
		Builds and Maintains Rapport with Client
		Proper Data Collection

Comments:

Sample Preference Assessment:

Stimulus Preference Assessment
Child Name:
Date:
Form Completed By:

What kind of **social praise** does your child enjoy? *Examples: tickles, smiles, hugs, high fives, thumbs up, compliments, flattery, whispers, shouts, handshake.*

On a scale of 1-5, with 5 being **always** enjoyable and 1 being **rarely** enjoyable please rate each activity listed above.

What kinds of **activities** does your child enjoy? *Examples: video games, board games, card games, riding a bike, watching a movie.*

On a scale of 1-5, with 5 being **always** enjoyable and 1 being **rarely** enjoyable please rate each activity listed above.

What kind of **objects/items** does your child enjoy? *Examples: stickers, markers, balloons, toy cars, baseball cards, marbles, Play Dough.*

On a scale of 1-5, with 5 being **always** enjoyable and 1 being **rarely** enjoyable please rate each activity listed above.

What kinds of **edibles/foods** does your child enjoy? *Examples: M&M's, ice cream, juice, soft textures, crunchy textures, peanut butter, cheese, salty, sweet, cold, sour.*

On a scale of 1-5, with 5 being **always** enjoyable and 1 being **rarely** enjoyable please rate each activity listed above.

What does your child most like to **see**? *Examples: items that spin, blink, flash, rock, rotate, move, jump, vibrate, shake, strobe lights.*

On a scale of 1-5, with 5 being **always** enjoyable and 1 being **rarely** enjoyable please rate each activity listed above.

What does your child most like to **hear**? *Examples: loud noises, soft noises, soothing sounds, arousing sounds, beeps, whistles, timers, horns, car noises, airplane noises, music.*

On a scale of 1-5, with 5 being **always** enjoyable and 1 being **rarely** enjoyable please rate each activity listed above.

What does your child most like to **touch**? *Examples: items that are wet, dry, soft, hard, cold, hot, firm, squishy, smooth, textured, furry.*

On a scale of 1-5, with 5 being **always** enjoyable and 1 being **rarely** enjoyable please rate each activity listed above.

What does your child most like to **smell**? *Examples: spices, fruity, sweet, musty, clean, sweaty, peppermint, lavender, licorice, cinnamon.*

On a scale of 1-5, with 5 being **always** enjoyable and 1 being **rarely** enjoyable please rate each activity listed above.

Sample Video/Audio Release Form:

<u>Photo/Video Release Form</u>

For the purposes of staff training, clinical supervision, advertisement, and/or to be included in promotional materials, photographs or video may be taken of the students engaging in therapy.

Please indicate below if you provide consent for your child to be photographed or videotaped. Photographs and video content will be stored in a confidential and secure manner, and are available for parent viewing at any time.

_____ I choose to **opt out** of allowing my child, _ (child name) __, to be photographed or videoed.

_____ I choose to **opt in** and allow my child, _ (child name) __, to be photographed or videoed for staff training/supervision purposes only.

_____ I choose to **opt in** and allow my child, _ (child name) __, to be photographed or videoed for staff training/supervision, and advertising or promotional use.

_____

Parent Printed Name

_____

Parent Signature

_____

Date

Sample Social Story:

<u>Nice Words</u>

When I use nice words to talk to people, it makes them happy.

Sometimes I forget to use my nice words. I might curse, tell someone I am going to hurt them, or yell at somebody.

It makes people feel bad when I don't use nice words.

Sometimes I want something I can't have, and I get upset. If I use nice words, I may get a chance to have it later!

Sometimes I feel angry, and I yell or forget to use nice words. If I use nice words like "I'm mad" or "I don't like that", an adult can help me calm down.

Calm Down

 take a deep breath

If I forget how to use nice words, I can ask my family or teacher to help me remember. I can say "Help me please".

If I whine, scream, or cry, people around me can get angry or upset.

If I use nice words and a calm voice, it makes people around me HAPPY!

Sample Manding Frequency Data Sheet:

Mand Frequency Data Sheet

Directions: Indicate the frequency of unprompted mands (U) vs. prompted mands (P). A prompted mand is a contrived situation, such as prompting the child to say "up" before you pick them up. An unprompted mand will spontaneously occur based on the child's motivation, such as if the child walks up to you and independently says "up". In a typical day, the child should be presented with several hundred opportunities to mand or roughly 25 opportunities per hour.

Date	Staff Initial	Unprompted	Prompted	What was the mand? *Please be specific. E.g. "Bah (bathroom)"

Sample Incidental Teaching Guidelines:

<u>Incidental Teaching-</u>
Setting: Natural Environments in or outside of home
Implemented by: Parents, Staff
Goals: See Incidental Teaching protocol
Procedure: Data is taken once per week during Cold Probes to assess mastery

Guidelines:
- Remember that Incidental Teaching is about capturing "teachable moments". You will need to follow the Jane Doe's interests and motivation.
- You need to prime the teaching environment. Set out Jane Doe's favorite toys and activities, create a rich environment of choices, allow her to briefly explore the items, and then begin teaching.
- Some days or sessions may vary in how many teachable moments you can capitalize on, this is normal. Some days Jane Doe will be less motivated than others.
- Create situations that resemble the natural environment as much as possible. If Jane Doe is learning to pull up a zipper, have her practice on her own coat and not on a doll.
- Mastery is determined through a Cold Probe.

Procedure:
- Prime the teaching environment for each teaching objective.
- Wait for Jane Doe to show interest in, reach for, or display curiosity about the teaching materials.
- After Jane Doe has initiated the incidental teaching episode, begin teaching the skill using a most to least prompting hierarchy. Use errorless teaching and do not allow Jane Doe to make errors. Block any incorrect response attempts (if physical).
- Provide differential verbal reinforcement depending upon the response. Tangible reinforcement is natural, meaning if Jane Doe is

learning to scoop ice cream into a bowl her reinforcer is eating the ice cream.

- Use descriptive praise, such as "Good job feeding the baby!" instead of just saying "Good job."
- End all teachable moments on a positive note, being sure to keep Jane Doe engaged and interested. Once Jane Doe loses interest, end the teaching session.
- Clear all teaching materials from the environment (as applicable) when all teaching trials are finished.

Sample Program:

Program Name: Tact to Intraverbal Transfer

Objective: John Doe will successfully transfer a known tact to an intraverbal. Example: John Doe correctly labels a photocard as a "dog". The photocard is removed and then he is asked "Tell me something that barks". John Doe responds "dog".

Materials: Photocards, objects

Prompting Procedure: Fully prompt all new targets. Unless you are 85% sure John Doe knows the skill, use the following prompting procedure-

Full prompt
Faded prompt
Distractor
Distractor
No prompt

SD: Present a known tact SD ("What is this?"), then remove the stimuli and present a novel intraverbal SD ("Tell me something that has feathers, its an animal, and it flies in the sky")

Mastery Criteria: John Doe must correctly make a tact –to- intraverbal transfer with no stimuli present, with 90% accuracy across 4 sessions

Target	Date Introduced	Date Mastered	Added to Maintenance Binder
Object prompt			Date:
Photo prompt			Date:

Full Verbal prompt			Date:
Partial verbal prompt			Date:
No prompt			Date:

Sample Program:

Program Name: Following an Activity Schedule

Objective: John Doe will be able to independently follow an activity schedule. Example: John Doe builds blocks, reads a book, and sorts laundry while checking his activity schedule to see what activity is next and smoothly transition between activities.

Materials: Activity schedule visual, various activities, timer

Prompting Procedure: Fully prompt all new targets. Unless you are 85% sure John Doe knows the skill, use the following prompting procedure-

Full prompt
Faded prompt
Distractor
Distractor
No prompt

Prompting Hierarchy: Physical prompting, modeling, verbal prompting, proximity, isolation

SD: "Time to check your schedule" or "Go check your schedule"

Mastery Criteria: Must perform skill across preferred and non -preferred activities, for a duration of at least 5 minutes per activity across home and school settings

Target	Date Introduced	Date Mastered	Added to Maintenance Binder
2 activities, 15 s each			Date:
2 activities, 30 s each			Date:
3 activities, 1 min each			Date:
3 activities, 90 s each			Date:
4 activities, 2 min each			Date:
4 activities, 5 min each			Date:
3-5 activities, 6 min each			Date:

Sample Receptive Language Teaching List:

Common Actions	Animals	Body Parts	Clothes	Categories
Eating	Cat	Eyes	Coat	People
Sleeping	Dog	Nose	Hat	Places
Running	Bird	Mouth	Jacket	Things
Cutting	Fish	Hair	Shirt	Actions
Drinking	Bear	Feet	Shoes	Animals
Jumping	Cow	Ears	Socks	Food
Coloring	Duck	Tongue	Button	Clothes
Washing	Tiger	Head	Pants	Toys
Kicking	Turtle	Legs	Belt	Vehicles
Reading	Chicken	Arms	Jeans	Furniture
Brushing	Elephant	Fingers	Boots	Drinks
Swinging	Frog	Teeth	Diaper	Fruits
Hugging	Horse	Thumbs	Dress	Musical instruments
Clapping	Lion	Toes	Pajamas	Tools
Swimming	Monkey	Neck	Underwear	Vegetables
Riding	Pig	Stomach	Shorts	Emotions
Lifting	Rabbit	Chest	Sweater	Colors
Holding	Sheep	Back	Glasses	Shapes
Knocking	Squirrel	Knees	Umbrella	Numbers
Throwing	Deer	Chin	Watch	Letters
Kissing		Fingernails		
Tickling				
Walking				
Closing				

Sample Intake Form:

<u>INTAKE FORM</u>

Parent's Name (s):

Address:

Contact Email Address:

Phone Number:

Child's Name:

 Age:

 DOB:

Siblings:

Special diet/Allergies:

Current Medications:

Grade:

School:

Diagnosis:

Date of Initial Diagnosis:

_____

Does child receive Speech Therapy, Physical Therapy, Occupational Therapy, Hippotherapy, etc.? If so, how often does child receive this therapy? :

Has child received ABA services previously? If so, when? :

Are there any current behavioral concerns and/or problem behaviors such as elopement, noncompliance, aggression, tantrums, throwing objects, self harming behaviors, etc.? If so, please estimate the number of times per day each behavior occurs. Please discuss:

Describe current eating and drinking patterns. Please indicate if child can feed self, what texture/types of foods he/she can eat. Also list if child is using sippy cups, bottles, or open mouth cups:

Describe sleeping patterns, sleeping schedule, bedtime, sleep consistently through night, etc:

Describe any current toileting issues, attempted toilet training instances, is child currently wearing diapers/pull ups/underwear, etc:

Please complete the following statement:

I am seeking ABA services for my child to receive assistance in the following areas:

_____

_____

_____

_____

Please list the four most critical skill deficits that you want your child to get help with. Number the items 1-4 with 1 being what is most important to you. For example: *1) Language, 2) Sibling Interaction, 3) Following Directions, & 4) Bedtime Routine.*

_____

_____

_____

_____

_____

Please describe your child's current functioning level in the following areas:

VOCAL IMITATION	Is skill currently present?	Is skill emerging, partially mastered, or fully mastered?
Sounds		
Words		
Simple Phrases		
Songs		
Complex Phrases		
Number Sequences		
SPONTANEOUS VOCALIZATIONS	Is skill currently present?	Is skill emerging, partially mastered, or fully mastered?
Spontaneous vocals		
Spontaneous imitation of words, or sounds		
Spontaneous requesting		
Spontaneous labeling		
PLAY & LESIURE SKILLS	Is skill currently present?	Is skill emerging, partially mastered, or fully mastered?
Explores toys in environment		
Plays with toys as they are designed		
Verbalizes while playing		
Plays interactively with peers		
Allows peers to be close during play		
Imitates peers during play		
Pretend play		
Has appropriate indoor		

play skills		
Has appropriate outdoor play skills		
SOCIAL INTERACTION	Is skill currently present?	Is skill emerging, partially mastered, or fully mastered?
Tolerates touch from peers		
Makes eye contact with peers		
Respond to peers		
Talks to peers		
Imitates peers		
Takes offered item from a peer		
Willingly shares items with peers		
Physically approaches and engages peers		
Will request a peer to do an activity (verbally or nonverbally)		
Asks for information		
Labels items for others		
Maintains attention of others		
DRESSING	Is skill currently present?	Is skill emerging, partially mastered, or fully mastered?
Can dress self with help		
Can dress self with no help		
Can adjust clothing as needed		
Can label clothing (verbally or nonverbally)		

EATING	Is skill currently present?	Is skill emerging, partially mastered, or fully mastered?
Can feed self with help		
Can feed self with no help		
Can keep area clean while eating		
Requests meals/snacks (verbally or nonverbally)		
TOILETING	Is skill currently present?	Is skill emerging, partially mastered, or fully mastered?
Is currently toilet trained, with help		
Is currently toilet trained, with no help		
Can remain dry throughout the day		
Will request the bathroom (verbally or nonverbally)		
Will urinate in toilet		
Will defecate in toilet		

Use this space to record any additional comments or questions you have:

Sample Parent Participation Policy:

<u>PARENT INVOLVEMENT POLICY</u>

Lack of parental involvement is detrimental to a child's development and progress within an ABA program. Many research studies have demonstrated that when parents are actively involved in their child's ABA therapy program, the results are increased developmental skills, improvements in progress, reduced conflict and stress inside of the home, and increased reports of marital satisfaction. The benefits of parental involvement in ABA therapy are varied and multiple, as are the detriments of a lack of parental involvement in ABA therapy.

The role of the ABA therapists, paraprofessionals, BCBA's, or BCaBA's, is to guide, oversee, and design programs, or to implement programs as a part of ABA therapy. The ultimate responsibility for the effectiveness, generalization, and maintenance of skills taught and behaviors reduced using ABA methodologies lies with the parents.

I have read the above statements regarding the empirical support for active parental involvement in ABA therapy.

Please Initial:
I ___ WOULD____WOULD NOT like a research article detailing the benefits of active parental involvement to be sent to me.

Please complete:

I have the following goals for my child during the time they are engaged in ABA therapy:

1.

_____

_____

2.

_____

_____

3.

_____

_____

I have the following goals for myself:

1.

_____

_____

2.

_____

_____

3.

_____

_____

I understand that active parental involvement is necessary and critical to the success of my child's ABA therapy. I will be held responsible for the goals I have listed on this document, and the Consultant agrees to help me remain committed to these goals, and modify these goals as may be necessary. Consistent and excessive instances of lack of active parental involvement on my part may result in a termination of the supervision contract, and a cessation of this working relationship. Lack of active parental involvement can include but is not limited to:

-Failure to maintain adequate communication, respond to requests for information, and submit required data (in any form) in a timely manner
-Failure to provide materials and accommodations for the ABA program (e.g., therapy room, materials, reinforcers, etc.)
-Failure to participate in recommended and applicable parent training and parent education as necessary for the success of the ABA program, and failure to appropriately seek out information and training about Autism & ABA
-Failure to monitor and stay on top of child's progress in ABA program, data records, and anecdotal data, failure to accurately convey this information to important stakeholders
-Failure to follow recommend treatment plans, skill acquisition programs, or behavior reduction plans as written and advised, and consistent and unapproved modifying of treatments plans, skill acquisition programs, or behavior reduction plans

_____   _____
Parent 1

_____   _____
Parent 2

_____
Program Director

_____
Date

Sample Explanations of Centers (for staff):

Procedure: Will vary depending on the Center. Each Center has unique goals to address and work on. Center activities can be done independently, with peers, or with the therapist. Each Center has a specified duration, use a timer to signify to Jane Doe when a Center is over. When the timer goes off Jane Doe should clean up the Center and move to the next one. Use a picture schedule to teach Jane Doe how to transition between Centers. When Jane Doe is unsure where to go next, refer her to the picture schedule.

Independent Play Skills-
Goals: Imaginative play, Solitary play, Parallel play, Cooperative play, Turntaking, Using language during play, Constructive Play
Procedure: Refer to Play Skills Program Data Sheets.

Reading area -
Goals: Independent reading, Group reading, Attending to a short story, Sight words, Letter ID, Word Decoding, Read to therapist, Word search activities, Match words to words, Match words to pictures, Letter sounds, Reading comprehension

Task Completion/ Work Stations-
Goals: Follows routine, Works independently on activities, Waits appropriately during transitions, Gets and returns own materials, Completes tasks in order, Informs therapist when finished with an activity, Requests help or assistance, Asks for needed materials to complete task, Academic tasks (reading, writing, spelling), Fine motor tasks (cutting, pasting, gluing), Vocational tasks (sorting silverware, folding clothes, stuffing envelopes)

Group Instruction-
Goals: Sitting appropriately in a group, Group attending, Following group instruction, 2 and 3 step commands, Raising hand, Raises hand and answers a question, Turn taking, Write on whiteboard, Read items off of

whiteboard, Use classroom materials (calendar, months of the year, etc), Generalized response forms

Tablework-
Setting: 1:1 intensive teaching in a minimally distracting area
Goals: Verbal Behavior Programs
Procedure: Refer to VB Teaching Procedure and current variable interval (VI). Data is taken once per week during Cold Probe. Anecdotal session notes are written at the end of each session.

NET-
Setting: Natural Environment in or outside of home
Goals: Generalize mastered skills. Refer to closed, maintenance, and mastered targets. Rotate between old and new mastered targets
Procedure: Refer to NET notes. Take anecdotal session notes combined with data

Sensory Play-
Setting: Inside and outside the home
Goals: Provide varied and exciting multi- sensory play options to Jane Doe such as water play, finger-painting, silly dancing to music, nature walks, etc.
Procedure: Refer to list of Sensory Play Checklist. Check off each activity as it is completed

Social Skills/Peer Interaction-
Setting: Various areas in the home, or the local park
Goals: Sharing, Turntaking, Greeting Others, Eye Contact, Conversation (vocal and nonvocal) Skills, Listening, Attending to a Speaker
Procedure: Include information about social skill play breaks and/or Outings in anecdotal session notes. Data is taken once per week during Cold Probe. As much as possible, include siblings or other children during social skills teaching time

Sample Toileting Task Analysis using Forward Chaining :

Toileting Data Sheet

Instruction: Provide an opportunity for John Doe to complete each step, in order. The active target is the first step (pull pants down). Provide prompting for all other steps. Indicate "I" for independent or "P" for prompted.

Date:						
Pull pants down						
Pull underwear down						
Sit on toilet 3 minutes						
Wipe genitals with 4 squares of tissue (if necessary)						
Wipe bottom with 4 squares of tissue (if necessary)						

Drop soiled tissue into toilet					
Pull underwear up					
Pull pants up					
Flush toilet					

Sample Social Story:

Zoo Social Story

Today at the zoo I am working for _____.

Every time I earn 3 tokens, I will get 5 minutes of
_____ when I get home.

If I do not earn any tokens at the zoo today, then I can not get
_____ when I get home.

I can earn tokens by having listening ears, staying close to Ms Tameika, using nice words and an inside voice, and having nice hands and feet.

Ms Tameika will tell me when I earn a token, I don't need to ask.

Sample Parent Training Document:

<u>Delivering a SD: Concise Instruction</u>

SD Definition: SD stands for discriminative stimulus. Think of the SD as the demand you give to your child, or questions you ask, that require a response. In a typical day you may deliver hundreds of SD's to your child that they may or may not respond to. It is important to become aware of the SD's you deliver so the child does not escape the demand, and it is important to learn how to deliver a SD properly.

- SD Guidelines:
  - Gain the child's attention
  - Deliver the SD in a clear, firm voice using minimal language
  - Observe closely to see if the child responds. If the child responds, provide reinforcement. If not, move directly into prompting.

Example-
  - Correct SD: *"It's time to clean up"*
  - Incorrect SD: *"I think you guys should start cleaning up now because dinner will be ready soon, oh yeah: what do you want for dinner?"*

Concise Instruction

- Concise instruction is about being clear about your expectations the <u>first</u> time, and teaching the child to be compliant with requests from an adult.
- Remember: SD's are given, not asked. If you ask a SD you are giving the child the option of refusal. Be sure to make your SD's a demand and not a question.

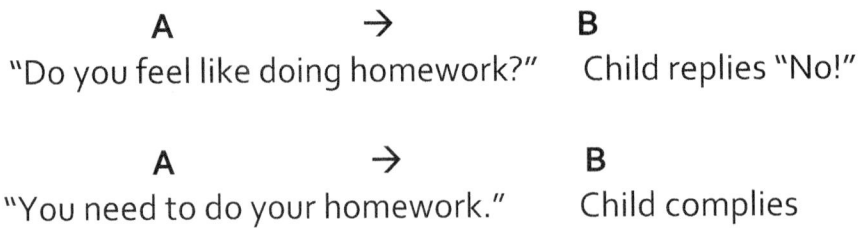

A	→	**B**
"Do you feel like doing homework?"		Child replies "No!"

A	→	**B**
"You need to do your homework."		Child complies

Try to make a habit out of delivering one SD at a time. Especially when dealing with a child who can be defiant or noncompliant, if you deliver a string of SD's at once it is likely the child won't do what you asked. Also, when you deliver one SD at a time you are increasing the number of opportunities the child has to contact reinforcement.

- *Is the SD always verbal?*
  - NO, sometimes a SD can be nonverbal. This could look like pointing to where the child should sit at the dinner table, or holding the child's coat open in front of them so they will put their coat on.

Sample Progress Report:

Child Name: Jane Doe

Program Start Date: June 1, 2012

Assessor: Program Director

-December 2012-

Jane is doing well with sitting for long period of times, and will now regularly sit for 2-10 minutes at a time. Jane is doing better at attending during therapy, and eye has improved. Jane has a Responding to Name program, and will now give eye contact within 4 seconds of her name being called. I am currently implementing a Picture Exchange Communication program with Jane, and she is on Phase I which requires her to hand me a picture of an item to receive access to that item. This is to eventually help her communicate her needs and wants. The Picture Exchange Communication program will also be implemented in the daycare setting soon, which will make it more effective.

Jane is not exhibiting any aggressive behaviors. The main behaviors Jane exhibits are noncompliance and elopement. The noncompliance seems to occur when Jane is presented with a challenging task or a demand she does not want to comply with. The elopement usually occurs when Jane is transitioning, such as from a break back to the table. Jane will sit down when prompted to do so, and may attempt to get right back up from the table. Jane benefits from gestural, and verbal, such as seeing the therapist point to her chair to indicate "sit down". Jane also benefits from consistent 3 step prompting, and her compliance has shown progress. Jane has a One Step direction program, and is currently working on sitting down upon demand. Jane's progress so far is inconsistent, and she can benefit from repeated instruction and varied reinforcement for this program.

Jane is continuing to work on identical matching, and is now matching objects with two distractors. She has mastered matching cards with up to three distractors. She should be able to increase the number of trials she does from 5 to at least 10-15 trials, and gradually introduce a field of 3. Jane is making great progress with her verbal programs, Vocal Imitation and Intraverbals. For Vocal Imitation, Jane will repeat a sound upon request. This has gotten very consistent in the past two weeks. For Intraverbals, Jane will make a sign for an English word using American Sign Language. Jane will also spontaneously say the word while she is signing. If Jane continues to make progress, she will eventually work on Echoics and Expressive Labeling. Jane has also begun making many spontaneous vocalizations within the past two weeks, and can imitate up to 7 simple words and phrases said to her during a session.

Jane is doing well with her Waiting program, and will now wait 15 seconds for a desired object or activity. Jane has built her way up to 15 seconds, starting with 5 seconds. Jane will eventually learn to wait for 3 minutes. Jane will consistently wait patiently during this program with her hands folder, and is usually quiet or hums to herself.

Jane is doing great working with puzzles, and has mastered large and small peg type puzzles. Jane is currently working on small inset puzzles, and is showing excellent progress. Jane is doing well with her Playing with Toys program, and can sit and attend to a toy for 3 minutes. This initially began as 1 minute. Jane is slightly inconsistent with this skill, and will sometimes give the toy or object back before the time is up. Jane is easily redirected to attend to the toy when this happens. The puzzle and toy programs will help when the Task Completion program is implemented. The Task Completion program will teach Jane leisure activities, which is a large concern of the family. Jane currently has no leisure skills and will wander the house if left unattended or engage in repetitive, self-stimulatory behaviors. The ability to sit and attend to a toy, and the skill of understanding puzzles will benefit the Task Completion program. The Task Completion program will likely be implemented in another 4-6 weeks.

Jane is doing better with her Receptive Language program, and has shown progress within the last week. Jane would not point to a card at all just a few weeks ago, and now will do so with an average of 40% accuracy.

Jane is doing great with Imitation using Objects. Jane has mastered tapping a table with a pen, and is now rolling a ball across a table. Jane will consistently imitate a simple motor activity using an object.

Jane is showing inconsistent progress with Category Sorting. Jane has been on the same target of sorting into 2 categories (animal, blank card) for a month, and her accuracy rate ranges from 30% to 50% on average. Jane will benefit from repeated instruction in sorting, and a possible substep to sorting using identical templates. If Jane does not show consistent progress in sorting within the next week, a substep will be introduced.

Jane will take a large amount of various objects when offered. Jane needs intensive services that continue to engage her and help her to learn communication skills, appropriate behavior in various situations, eye contact and focusing/attention skills. She is continuing to make progress with feeding. She is not making progress with urinary toilet training, and the home environment has placed toilet training on hold for the moment. Staff will be providing the family with instruction and resources for toilet training and helping them create a personalized toileting schedule for Jane . The parents are going to review the information, and decide if they are ready to pursue in-home toilet training intensively.

Transition Plan:

Once Jane masters the ABLLS assessment grid, then she can decrease ABA services to 5-8 hours a week. She currently receives 15 hours of therapy each week, with 2 hours of Parent Education training provided outside of therapy. After six months, if Jane shows no regression or loss of mastery, then she can decrease her hours to 8-12 hours a week. We would continue to work on expanding her vocabulary to a more age appropriate level, and providing support and education to the family. When she shows that she is able to mainstream into a typical classroom with typical peers and is able to complete her work at grade level, then she can decrease her hours to zero. If she has any problem behaviors that arise after that point, then it can be dealt with on a consultation basis as needed. It would be important that her teachers are trained on how to work with her within an ABA model to ensure her continued progress and success, and that the family continues to use a consistent behavioral plan with Jane.

Current Active Programs:

-Skill: PECS: Picture Exchange Communication System
Current Target: Phase 1, Known Reinforcers

Objective: Jane will learn to give over a picture card of an item to receive the actual item.

-Skill: Waits without touching stimuli
Current Target: Objective 1

Objective: When an instructor is attempting to engage Jane in learning activities (at a table, while seated on the floor, or standing near materials for an activity), Jane will wait calmly, remain generally oriented towards the instructor and materials, and will keep her hands away from the instructional materials until an instruction is presented.
2= While sitting or standing in front of task materials Jane consistently waits calmly orienting towards the materials without requiring prompts to leave the materials alone
1= requires only one prompt to sit/stand nicely or keep hands off the materials

-Skill: Puzzles with multiple connecting pieces in an inset-type frame
Current Target: Objective 2
Mastered: Objective 1

Objective: When given uniquely-shaped, connecting puzzle pieces which fit into an irregularly shaped inset frame, Jane will complete the puzzle.
4= 4 puzzles with 8 pieces
3= 4 puzzles with 5 pieces
2= 2 puzzles with 5 pieces
1= 1 puzzle with at least 5 pieces

-Skill: Imitates sounds on request
Current Target: Objective 1

Objective: Jane will imitate a sound when you say,"Say ___"

4= readily and accurately imitates almost any sound
3= 15 sounds
2= 5 sounds
1= 2 sounds

-Skill: Plays with toys/ manipulates toys as designed
Current Target: Objective 1

Objective: Jane will actively play with toys as designed
2= plays with at least two toys as designed without prompts for up to 10 minutes
1= plays with at least one toy as designed for up to 10 minutes with occasional prompts.

-Skill: Sign English words using American Sign Language
Current Target: Objective 1

Objective: Jane will be able to provide a sign (American Sign Language (ASL) when given an English word
4= 25 signs
3= 15 signs

2= 5 signs
1= 2 signs

-Skill: Specific motor responses in receptive tasks
Current Target: Objective 1

Objective: Jane will select common objects and pictures with a specific motor response when given a variety of instructions specifying the response required to select those items (e.g., "Touch," "Point to," "Give me," "Pick up," "Get the").
4= responds correctly to any of 5 different selection responses
3= four different selection responses
2= three different selection responses
1= two different selection responses

-Skill: Motor imitation using objects
Current Target: Objective 1

Objective: Upon request, Jane will imitate a motor activity with an object. Will Jane imitate a motor action using an item/object when asked to "Do this"?
4= at least 10 actions with at least two different actions for each object
3= 10 actions
2= 5 actions
1= 2 actions

-Skill: Sort non-identical items
Current Target: Objective 1

Objective: When given a variety of non-identical objects or pictures representing three items, and given an array of sample items for each of the three items, Jane will sort non-identical items into the appropriate groups (e.g., all the dogs, all the trees, all the people).

4= given 20 items (5 each of 4 items)
can sort 10 or more types of items into an array of 4 samples
3= given 12 items (3 each of 4 items)
can sort at least 6 types of items into array of 4 samples
2= given 6 items (2 each of 3 items)
can sort at least 4 types of items into array of 3 samples
1= given 4 items (2 each of 2 items)
can sort 2 types of items into an array of 2 samples

-Skill: Responds to own name
Current Target: Objective 1

Objective: Jane will look at or come to a person when called by her name.
2= looks or comes at least 80% of the time
1= requires some prompts to respond

-Skill: Match identical objects to sample
Current Target: Objective 2
Mastered: Objective 1

Objective: When given an object, Jane will match to an identical object in an array of three items.
4= at least 10 objects to objects in a display of 8 items
3= at least 5 objects to objects in a display of 4 items
2= at least two objects to objects in a display of 2 items
1= can match one object to an identical object in a display of 2 items

-Skill: Follow instructions to do a simple motor action
Current Target: Objective 1

Objective: Will Jane follow an instruction to do a simple motor action upon request (e.g., "Clap hands")?

4= at least 6 instructions without prompts and can follow at least 4 different actions within 10 seconds

 3= at least 6 instructions without prompts

2= at least 4 instructions without prompts

1= at least 2 instructions without prompts Jane will comply with instructions to do a simple motor task (e.g., clap, turn around, arms up).

Printed in Great Britain
by Amazon

47012774R00066